ISBN: 9798793026215
First published: 2022
Copyright: Alex Warren, 2022

Special thanks to Sanjay Dove, Debby Penton and the whole
Wildfire team

Cover design by Liam Jackson Graphics

In 1909 E.M. Forster wrote The Machine Stops. At barely 12,000 words, the award-winning novella has inspired sci-fi writers and technologists ever since.

The story describes a future in which human beings have lost the ability to live above ground, being kept alive through an interconnected underground 'Machine'.

What I've always loved about Forster's work is that, while the novella is clearly dystopian, there is no robot revolution. There's no clear tipping point, no uprising, and no reference to any one moment when the world changed. Instead, with every passing year, Forster's inhabitants have simply grown more accustomed to working within the confines of the Machine, serving it with "increased efficiency and decreased intelligence."

Despite being published more than 100 years ago Forster's novella can still tell us a lot about our relationship with technology.

For all the fears of algorithms outsmarting us, robots stealing our jobs, and even an AI apocalypse, the reality is that technology's impact is much more mundane. While there may be the occasional burst of innovation, it's the incremental changes, the daily ground we concede, that defines the long-term impact on our lives.

SPIN MACHINES

Robots, revolutions, and the future of the PR agency

1.

Spinners and losers

As a profession, public relations is terrible at keeping up with the times.

Whatever the latest trend is, PR professionals can usually be found lagging six months behind. Analytics, digital marketing, influencer relations, SEO, you name it; as an industry we're always playing catch up with our friends over in advertising and marketing.

Maybe it's because of the vague nature of what we do. Where both marketing and advertising have a rich history of cool and creative success stories, PR lacks confidence in its role. Everyone remembers their favourite advert, but how many people can tell you their favourite PR campaign?

This lack of confidence means PR professionals have argued for years about even the most basic aspects of what we do. Does PR actually work? How do we define it? Can it be measured? Where does our role end and the role of marketing begin?

Unable to answer even these most basic questions, the public relations industry tends to fall back on what it feels comfortable with — something that typically means an overreliance on media relations.

While marketers are experimenting with new targeting technologies and advertisers are exploring the very latest trends, PR agencies continue to pester journalists, churn out press releases and organise wacky stunts. It's hardly the most sophisticated stuff.

And it's not just tactics that are behind the times. The structure at the heart of most PR agencies has also barely changed. The world's largest (and supposedly best) agencies still rely on hierarchical structures, bloated boards and an army of low-level account executives frantically hitting the phones.

This is one of the reasons why PR has been consistently ranked as one of the world's most stressful jobs.[1] Uncertain of their ability to add real, measurable business value, PR agencies adopt a 'just say yes' attitude, often overpromising and underdelivering on a whole host of tasks that junior teams haven't been appropriately trained to deliver.

It's in this environment that PR becomes a catch all for other people's jobs. From events management to copywriting, digital marketing to graphics design, PR agencies love to scoop up tactical tasks that distract from what they should be doing... *genuinely strategic PR.*

This panicked, catch-all mentality has put PR permanently on the back foot. When important developments arise, too many of us miss, shirk, or simply ignore them.

That's why I wanted to write this book. I believe that PR agencies around the world are about to face one of the biggest revolutions our industry has ever seen. I also believe that we, as PR professionals, are once again horribly ill prepared.

I'm of course talking about artificial intelligence (AI) and the pending inevitable role it'll play in disrupting, automating and rewriting the future of our profession.

And yes, I know the PR industry has been talking about the 'disruptive potential' of AI for almost a decade. But in that time, what have we done about it? What have we done to protect and prepare our industry for this unprecedented change? Nothing.

Now, I should say at this point that this book isn't some apocalyptic manifesto. I'm well aware that any talk about AI 'taking over' industries immediately conjures images of Terminator-style robots forcing PR pros out of their jobs. That's not what I'm talking about. What I want to address is the very strong possibility that *most low-level PR functions are about to be automated out of existence.*

This inevitable automation poses both one of the biggest threats and, I believe, one of the biggest opportunities for the PR industry — especially PR agencies.

Agencies that want to survive (and ideally thrive) in an increasingly automated world need to dramatically rethink the way their businesses are currently structured. They also need to take a long hard look at the sort of work they deliver for clients and what it means to be a PR consultant. Unfortunately, the slow-moving nature of the public relations industry makes it far more likely that we'll fail to prepare for (or even take advantage of) this inevitable shift.

But then again, perhaps we don't need to worry. As an industry focused on building human relationships, it's easy to assume that PR is somehow exempt from the coming tidal wave of automation and AI.

I disagree.

I've always thought there's something snobbish about

assuming we're above automation. We like to think it's only factory workers, lorry drivers and blue-collar jobs that machines will ever replace. But not us. Not the middle-class creative types. Not the people sitting on beanbags brainstorming ideas to get our clients in *The Guardian*. We're convinced our work is far too clever, too creative, and too unstructured to ever be palmed off on an algorithm.

I want to dispel that myth, and to remind PR professionals — and agencies in particular — that there has never been a better time to prepare for radical disruption.

At the rate that artificial intelligence is evolving it's exactly these types of unstructured, creative jobs that will be most at risk over the next 10 years. In the following pages I want to remind PR professionals of that fact, as well as help agencies prepare for the potentially turbulent decade ahead.

While right now, automated public relations might be focused on press release distributions, media monitoring and list creation, all of these small changes will eventually lead to something bigger. Even if AI doesn't directly replace our jobs, the ongoing automation of low-level tasks is going to have serious ramifications for the structure of traditional PR firms.

The need for armies of account executives is inevitably going to shrink, with AI bringing increased efficiency and allowing more day-to-day work to be performed with a far smaller team.

Faced with these changes, agency bosses will have to make a choice. Do they fire these individuals and reduce the size of their agencies? Do they repurpose this additional free time for yet more pitching and media relations? Or do they use it as an opportunity to retrain these individuals and look for entirely new ways to add value to clients?

This book will argue for the latter as well as considering the very likely possibility that artificial intelligence will not just replace the most mundane PR tasks, but also the most rewarding (from media relations to copywriting, and even creativity itself).

None of this falls within the realms of science fiction. Every technology discussed is either something that already exists or is in development. All of it will require serious consideration from PR agencies in the next 10 to 15 years.

While a lot of what will be discussed in the following chapters could be applied to both PR agencies and in-house roles, it's worth saying that this book focuses heavily on the impact of automation on public relations *agencies*.

In many ways, it will be agencies that are worst hit. Not only will they have to contend with automation within their own businesses, but also the impact that automation will have on their clients. Low-cost automation will bring more PR functions in house, lowering budgets and reducing the need to hire external agencies. Either way, the agency model will need to adjust dramatically.

A final point worth making is a quick note on terminology.

Despite the catchy, alliterative subtitle about robots and revolutions, there will in fact be little talk of robotics. This is a book about software-based automation, algorithms and the potential of AI in the context of public relations. Given this focus, it's fair to say that I won't be going into a lot of tedious technical details about artificial intelligence itself (beyond a few handy definitions in the next chapter). Following these definitions, the rest of this book is split into three parts:

The first identifies the problems facing PR agencies over the next 10 years. It discusses the growth of automation in other industries and why PR professionals have been so slow to consider AI as anything more than a buzzword with limited impact on their roles.

The second looks at the core elements of public relations that AI and automation will one day replace. For the most part, this focuses on the elements of agency life that we've told ourselves machines cannot replicate — from creativity to writing, strategy and media relationships.

Finally, in part three, I've laid out my vision for how agency life could evolve, and how PR could be at the start of a trend rather than the end of it.

To conclude, I've provided a five-step 'survival guide' for the future of the PR agency, explaining how an informed, bold, and consultancy-based approach could help turn this upcoming threat into a serious opportunity.

Before we jump into any of that though, there's one question that I fear will come up a lot so probably needs to be addressed... what the hell is AI?

2.

What the hell is AI?

Many a marketer has found themselves down a rabbit hole when trying to explain the more technical details of artificial intelligence, and I'm no exception.

When researching this chapter, I discovered that there are 14 types of machine learning alone, ranging from transfer learning to ensemble learning. So, to clarify, I have no intention of explaining all of the different types of coding structures involved in building your own AI. What I will do, however, is use the next couple of pages to at least explain the key terms that PR professionals might end up coming across in their day-to-day work (or in the remainder of this book).

Big data: Big data is essentially a useful term for extremely large data sets typically analysed by a computer to reveal patterns, trends and associations. Big data isn't AI, but it has proved very handy for making AI possible.

These days, almost everything we do gives off bags of data, all of which is recorded and stored. Big data comes from our music preferences on Spotify, our travel habits on TripAdvisor, even the brushing routines from our internet-connected toothbrushes. This all adds up to giant, dispersed datasets known as big data.

While the concept of big data has been around for decades, it was always impossible to analyse such vast data manually. As such, automation was needed, which brings us nicely onto our next AI buzzword.

Automation: Automation can apply to anything. It's basically the use of machines to minimise human effort or labour, often supplementing or even taking over human practices, processes and professions.[2] Traditionally, automation was associated with hardware and machines, such as the automation of manual labour within factories (think robot arms building cars). These days though, automation is just as likely to occur through software, with *algorithms* being used to automate decisions and activities that would once have been conducted by a person sitting at a computer. So, what's an algorithm?

Algorithm: Algorithms are procedures or formulae for solving particular problems, typically based on conducting a sequence of specified actions.[3] They're basically a set of guidelines that describe how to perform a task — think flow diagrams or a cheat sheet.

Computers follow these algorithms to achieve everything from targeting advertising to playing the stock exchange, right down to delivering your favourite pizza.

Of all the explanations I've seen, I think the mathematician Marcus du Sautoy did the best job of explaining algorithms:

"An algorithm exploits the pattern underlying the way we solve a problem to guide us to a solution. The computer doesn't need to think. It just follows the instructions encoded in the algorithm again and again, and, as if by magic, out pops the answer you were looking for."[4]

Artificial intelligence (AI): This is where people start to get confused. Artificial intelligence is not a specific technology. If anything, it's really more of an end result than a method for getting there.[5] AI describes the thing we're trying to achieve — the simulation of human intelligence by machines. At its most basic, this could mean machines that simply mimic humans based on their past behaviours. At its most advanced, it could mean machines that are conscious, feeling or even smarter than humans.[6]

The academic Noam Lemelshtrich Latar makes a handy distinction to separate AI from previous technologies. According to Latar, we've already lived through 'augmented intelligence', where computers help people with their day-to-day tasks (think the rise of personal computing in the 1990s). More recently we've had 'collective intelligence' where machines brought together the world's minds all in one place (the internet). Finally, we'll have artificial intelligence, where human beings create a form of consciousness that even they can't fully understand. This is the ultimate vision for AI. Moving from augmented decisions to collective decisions and finally to autonomous decisions.[7]

It's worth mentioning at this point that AI isn't quite there yet. Right now, AI is still used as little more than an umbrella term for various technologies with a similar goal.[8] There have been dozens of individual technologies and processes developed to achieve artificial intelligence, and these are all broadly grouped under the (somewhat unhelpful) term AI. Common examples include voice recognition (machines that appear to respond to speech), affective computing (machines that mimic human emotions) and robotics (machines that physically act like humans). Perhaps the most popular form of AI right now, is machine learning.

Machine learning (ML): Machine learning sits under the AI umbrella and is currently one of the most popular ways to imitate human intelligence within machines. Probably the best (simplest) definition I've found for machine learning comes from Jim Sterne, author of *AI for Marketing*. He defines it as computers that are "designed to learn, not to follow strict rules."[9]

This is the essence of how machine learning works. Rather than following a strict set of instructions like a traditional algorithm, machine learning is set a broad goal and has the freedom to work out the very best way to achieve it. Avinash Kaushik, digital marketing evangelist at Google (yes, that is his real job title) has further expanded on this definition saying, "AI is an intelligent machine and ML is the ability to learn without being explicitly programmed."[10]

At this point the so-called 'learning' in ML is largely achieved through big data. By throwing a huge amount of information at ML algorithms they can identify patterns and use these patterns to build — and ultimately test — their own hypotheses.

Take, for instance, the classic example of using machine learning to identify the difference between photographs of cats and dogs.

To begin, you would start with a pair of large, labelled data sets. Let's say, 50,000 photos of cats (labelled 'cat') and 50,000 photos of dogs (labelled 'dog'). Feeding these images into the machine, the algorithm can look for similarities between each and test its own hypothesis of what makes a cat and what makes a dog. It doesn't have to rely on a preprogramed method; it purely has the goal of splitting the images into two clear categories.

To start with, it may identify that all the cats have four legs before quickly learning that dogs also have four legs, making this a poor point of differentiation. After a few tries however, it may identify that all the cats have pointy ears. This could provide the basis for a simple hypothesis — cats have pointy ears, dogs don't. Once this is established, future *unlabelled* images can be imported into the machine for identification. Using the self-composed idea that cats have pointy ears and dogs don't, the machine learning algorithm could then identify which photos contain cats and which contain dogs with a far greater degree of accuracy.

Once this guess has been confirmed by humans, the algorithms can start to add more layers of data to make their predictions even more accurate.

Say for example that the machine comes across an image of a chihuahua. Unlike many dogs, chihuahuas do have pointy ears, meaning that under the current hypothesis they would be identified incorrectly as a cat. Once this error has been identified by the human operator, the machine can set about adding another layer of analysis. One example could be that cats have both pointy ears *and* long tails. This hypothesis would correctly place the chihuahua in the dog category. As more data goes in and more trials run, machine learning gets smarter and smarter, ultimately reaching complex conclusions with no visible instructions or coding on the part of the human programmer.

Deep learning / neural networks: Ok, so we've got AI — the umbrella term for machines that think or act like people. Next, we've got ML — the most common way of achieving AI through algorithms that develop themselves. Finally, there's deep learning.

Deep learning is a subset of ML in which numerous layers of machine learning algorithms are run on top of one another. These algorithms are created by building up layers of questions that can help reach a conclusion. They're commonly called neural networks because they mimic the way the human brain works. In short, each of these ML algorithms tests a different hypothesis or provides a different interpretation of the data it feeds on. The result is something far closer to the complex, naturalistic decision making achieved by human beings.

Deep learning has proved especially powerful for those more complex elements of artificial intelligence, such as replicating creativity, intuition or interpersonal decision making. Unfortunately, much in the same way we struggle to understand how human creativity or intuition comes about, the problem with such advanced deep learning systems is that they are increasingly opaque.[11] Those who designed these systems are losing sight of how the resulting decisions are being made, and that poses a serious conundrum for their ethical adoption in society.

Beneath these high-level definitions there are a whole host of different subcategories surrounding AI. For the purposes of this book, however, the above are probably the only terms you'll really need to know. As far as the PR industry is concerned, it's machine learning — and increasingly deep learning — that represents the biggest opportunity, and the biggest threat, to the existing PR agency model.

PART 1

"If there is one myth regarding computer technology that ought to be swept into the dustbin, it is the pervasive belief that computers can do only what they are specifically programmed to do."

— Martin Ford, AI futurist[12]

3.

The robots are here

Whether it's economists, futurists, or just good old-fashioned psychics, many of us are rightly distrusting of people who claim to predict the future. As such, when I make claims about PR agencies fundamentally changing (or even disappearing) within 15 years, I can see why you might be sceptical.

To me though, talking about AI in this way isn't about predicting the future, it's about looking at the past. So much of what artificial intelligence can do (or is likely to disrupt) is already on display. The machines aren't coming, they're already here; you just need to look at the industries that are ahead of PR on the adoption curve.

Take the recycling industry as just one example.

Five years ago, the world was producing just under 400 million tonnes of plastic waste, with the vast majority ending up in the world's oceans.[13] One of the biggest challenges faced by this industry has been the manual (human) processes involved in sorting rubbish and deciding which items can or can't be recycled. In recent years, AI has overhauled this process. Where a human sorter would be able to identify and pick out around 30 items per minute, robots incorporating AI such as SamurAI or RoCycle can easily pick upwards of 80 items per minute.[14]

In the last year, new technology, which mixes infrared light and a system of chains and magnets, is sorting up to three thousand recyclable objects per minute.[15]

It's this type of blue-collar work that the combination of AI and automation has already revolutionised. And it's not likely to stop there. While it sounds like science fiction, some of the world's greatest minds are seriously looking at how AI can replace the majority of the planet's jobs and workforces.[16] Scholars at the University of Oxford estimate that no less than 47% of all American jobs and 54% of those in Europe are at a high risk of being usurped by machines.[17] Another Oxford study, *The Future of Jobs*, suggested that millions of workers in the UK are in danger of being replaced by computers, algorithms and machines.[18]

Looking at 702 popular professions the study assigned a probability of computerisation to each occupation, ranking from 0% (no risk of automation) to 100% (very high risk). Of course, the irony of this study was that — when it came to the heavy mathematics — most of the human academics involved weren't really required, with a set of algorithms ultimately being used to calculate and assign the probabilities.[19]

Of the 702 professions analysed, the following were all assigned a 99% probability of being automated in future: data entry keyers, library technicians, new accounts clerks, photographic process workers, processing machine operators, tax preparers, cargo and freight agents, watch repairers, insurance underwriters, mathematical technicians, title examiners and telemarketers.[20]

These may sound niche, but remember, these are the professions that scored a 99% certainty of automation. Those scoring about 70% included hundreds more blue-collar jobs across all variety of professions.

For these jobs, AI algorithms and automation don't have to mean total destruction. While almost all professions are susceptible to automation, the majority are only partially automatable right now. The McKinsey Global Institute estimates that 60% of all occupations have at least 30% automatable activities.[21] So even if a job isn't replaceable, a significant chunk of the day-to-day work will be automated out of existence.

We should also be prepared for this figure to grow dramatically and suddenly over the next 15 years because of what technologists and AI professionals have called the 'ketchup effect'.[22] In short, technology adoption acts like ketchup sliding out of a glass bottle — first nothing, then a drip and then half the bottle comes crashing out seemingly all at once.

We've seen this effect in action with other technologies. Ideas that have been around for years get tweaked or finished, or even just repackaged, and suddenly they become unstoppable.

Look at ebooks. The idea of electronic books has been around for decades, with the first ever e-reader seeing its release in 1971 (admittedly it could only read the declaration of independence).[23] For years, big players in the tech world toyed with the idea of creating e-readers and supporting ebook libraries, but the vision never quite became a reality. Then, in 2007, Amazon launched the Kindle and the entire ketchup bottle came gushing out. In under five years, the number of ebooks being sold on Amazon surpassed both the number of paperbacks and hardbacks combined.[24] Kobo and other competitors also joined the market, and soon seeing someone holding an e-reader was no longer 'futuristic' but just a mundane reality of the modern world.

AI will be no different. Yes, it feels like everyone has been talking about the power of AI forever with only limited visible results. But to my mind, we're still in the drip phase. AI technologies are having a huge impact, but only on very specific tasks and very specific fields. Blue-collar jobs have been the hardest hit and will almost certainly continue to be hit over the next few years.

But what about for white-collar professions like public relations? Returning to the University of Oxford's *Future of Jobs* study, of the 702 professions labelled at risk of automation, public relations ranked 634th.

At this point, PR professionals breathed a sigh of relief. Clearly our jobs are just too unique, too creative, and too irreplaceably human to ever automate.

Yeah right.

4.

We're safe

With public relations scoring so low on the list of at-risk professions, it's been far easier for the industry to bury its head in the sand, assuming that automation will impact everyone else, but not us.

The problem with this mindset, particularly within white-collar industries, is that nobody thinks that their particular skillset could ever be replaced.

In their book *The Future of the Professions*, Daniel and Richard Susskind observe this phenomenon almost universally.[25] It doesn't matter if you're speaking to a lawyer, architect, business professional or marketer, the view is always the same: automation would be wonderfully effective at replacing any task in almost any field... just not *my* bit.

That type of thinking doesn't just apply to automation either. It's pretty much applicable to any tech-based streamlining or radical industry change. When it comes to their livelihoods — and their areas of expertise — people are immensely reluctant to change. They also find it extremely difficult to visualise new ways of doing things.[26]

There are two possible reasons for this. The first is a grandiose sense of self-worth. "My job is far too complicated for an unthinking machine to replace."

All of us tend to *overestimate* how difficult our jobs are and *underestimate* how difficult the jobs of others are. As such, when it comes to evaluating whether a profession could be streamlined or even automated out of existence, those closest to the profession can be some of the worst to judge.

The second, and perhaps more cynical possibility, is that many white-collar professionals do see the potential for automation within their jobs but simply don't admit it. As Richard Susskind puts it in *The Future of the Professions*:

"Professions do not themselves generally want to change, and so resist reform or revolution... to what extent do we actually trust professionals to admit that their services could be delivered differently, or that some of their work could responsibly be passed along to non-professionals? If we leave it to professionals themselves to reinvent their workplace, are we asking the rabbits to guard the lettuce?"[27]

Personally, I don't think PR people are lying when they say they see little possibility for AI to replace them in their jobs. I do, however, think that they both *overestimate* the difficulty of their work and *underestimate* the rate at which artificial intelligence is evolving.

After nearly 10 years in the industry, I'm quite happy to confess that we PR people love to make our work sound more complicated (and more stressful) than it is. Half of the magic of PR comes from convincing people you have these deep-seated bonds and special relationships with journalists and influencers. We love to promote the idea that we've got a little black book of contacts, full of influential people who are at our beck and call following years of networking and relationship building. In reality, that's rarely the case.

Most PR agencies today have Google, Twitter and a paid-for media contacts database. Yes, we all have a handful of favourite journalists or influencers who we once got pissed with at a Christmas party, but that's about as far as it goes.

The truth is that journalists are very busy. They're overwhelmed with potential stories to write and they'll virtually never write about something that they (and their readers) don't find interesting. No amount of networking, schmoozing or special relationships is ever going to change that. There is no dark art to media relations; most of it's just a case of finding the slim central crossover in the Venn diagram of what your client wants to talk about and what journalists want to write.

Still, nobody wants to admit that. The need to make PR sound complex and Machiavellian runs deep in the industry. Just take the writings of Ryan Holiday, PR influencer and former spin doctor at American Apparel:

"I am, to put it bluntly, a media manipulator — I'm paid to deceive. My job is to lie to the media so they can lie to you."[28]

While not everyone is as direct as Ryan Holiday, talk of psychology, persuasive storytelling, consumer profiling and media influence abounds throughout the industry. The result is a straightforward profession made to sound like a dark art, a complex science, or both.

But while PR may not at heart be that complex, I can at least admit that it is extremely varied. The best PR professionals receive the (fairly substantial) wages they do because their skillset is incredibly mixed. To be successful in PR you need to be a good writer, a good storyteller, good with people, well organised, a great public speaker, an events organiser and a good project manager. You must also take on the role of a journalist, a strategist, a tactician, a social media guru and a research data nerd all at once.

To confuse things even more, there is no single 'rinse-and-repeat' process for PR. What worked for one brand won't necessarily work for another. In fact, it won't even work for the same brand a second time around. Your creative campaign that secured national TV coverage one day may deliver nothing at all the next. Even more frustrating, the thing that made your client so happy yesterday might make them seethe with rage today. Agency life is a minefield.

Given all this, it's easy to see why PR pros feel safe in the knowledge that their profession will never be automated out of existence. Machines have a habit of replacing things that follow clear repeatable patterns. If your job involves putting the same nut onto the same bolt or pressing the same buttons and pulling the same levers every day, there's a good chance that an algorithm (or maybe even a physical robot) is coming for you. If, however, you go into work each morning genuinely unsure of what your day is going to look like, then you've probably got a little bit of a wait.

That wait, however, may not be as long as we all hope.

The reason that simple and repetitive jobs have traditionally been replaced by machines is that, up until this point, the algorithms behind those machines have been equally simple and repetitive. Traditional computer algorithms have followed predictable formulae, such as conditional statements ('if, then, else').

By pre-programming a series of instructions, and conditions for when those instructions should be implemented, any simple repetitive task can be quite easily replaced by an automated system.

While the mathematics behind these algorithms has grown increasingly complex, computer scientists have also become better at breaking seemingly complex tasks down into bite-sized chunks. This way, a whole host of tasks — and professions — that seemed incredibly complicated on the surface can be performed by layer upon layer of relatively simplistic code.

What this formulaic code cannot do, however, (no matter how many layers of it are piled on top of one another) is generate new ideas — to 'think' or act creatively. In this type of structured programming, it is down to the programmers to think and the machines to follow orders. But with artificial intelligence, all this is changing.

As described in chapter 2, AI does not really think for itself, but it does at least create original concepts. AI can be used to identify patterns that no human would have seen, to optimise plans, generate new content and even 'brainstorm' new ideas. The code behind AI is not fixed, making it far more likely to replace traditional human tasks, jobs and entire professions. As digital historian Yuval Noah Harari puts it:

"Manufacturing jobs and labour-intensive occupations harbouring hefty volumes of repetitious tasks will likely be the first to experience severe disruption. But as machine learning becomes increasingly intelligent in shorter periods of time, professions that require complex cognitive and social-emotional skills might soon follow."[29]

So, has AI reached a point where it could theoretically, or even practically, replace a creative, unstructured profession like PR? To understand this potential turning point, let's take a brief tangent to consider the Chinese strategy game, Go.

In 1997, IBM's Deep Blue AI beat world champion Garry Kasparov in a pair of six-game chess matches.[30] While this was a big step forward for AI, the structured, rules-based nature of chess does make it easier for computers to learn and play. Go, on the other hand, is a much more abstract undertaking, with seemingly irrelevant moves having huge and unexpected consequences for players later on in the game. A rules-based approach simply will not work for Go. Or, if it does, those same rules cannot be applied in future games.[31]

Given this fact, most pundits at the time of Deep Blue's win predicted that it would be generations before an AI could take on one of the world's greatest Go grandmasters, with astrophysicist Piet Hut writing at the time: "It may be a hundred years before a computer beats humans at Go — maybe even longer."[32]

So, did it take one hundred years?

Of course not. A mere 18 years later, Google's AlphaGo became the first computer to beat a Go grandmaster without a handicap. Since then, the algorithm has gone on to beat multiple world champions — before finally retiring and being replaced by the superior AlphaGo Zero.[33]

Obviously, most of us have no intention of becoming a Go grandmaster. Likewise, the automation of Go players probably isn't set to have a huge effect on PR, marketing or the wider economy. Still, it's important to talk about this example as a turning point for AI. Go was a game that everyone thought would take hundreds of years to effectively automate — 20 years later, it's already done.

The rapidly approaching reality is that, with enough time, data and processing power, almost any task can be performed by machines. The fact that public relations is considered near the bottom of the list shouldn't make us feel any safer or more smug than those at the top.

For a potentially more practical example, just look at automated vehicles. In 2004 (long before Oxford's *Future of Jobs* study), professor Frank Levy from MIT and professor Richard Murnane from Harvard published their own study, listing the professions most and least likely to be automated in the future.

In their summary, Levy and Murnane cited truck drivers as a clear example of a job that could not possibly be automated in future.[34] The sheer complexity involved in driving a vehicle, navigating endless roads, obeying traffic laws and making snap judgments to avoid a crash was simply impossible for an algorithm to replicate.

And now, here we are. Not even two decades later and self-driving vehicles are a reality. From Google to Tesla, self-driving cars not only exist but are actually being allowed on the road.[35] At the time of writing there are almost 2,000 autonomous vehicles in operation around the world, including UPS's fleet of self-driving trucks.[36] Sorry truck drivers.

It would be crazy to pretend that the road to fully autonomous vehicles is a short one. A couple of thousand cars and a fleet of trucks originally launched as a PR stunt isn't exactly evidence of seismic societal change. Still, the technology does exist, the rules of use are being written, and the path to a driverless future is increasingly clear. Just like ebooks, the iPhone, Uber or digital streaming services, we must remember to watch out for that infamous ketchup effect. First nothing, then a drip and then half the bottle.

In the space of 10 years, we very quickly go from questioning technologies we've never heard of to struggling to imagine our lives without them. The automation of work, whether that be driving trucks or running a PR agency, may very soon be the same.

5.

Automating the boring bits

While there may be a big difference between driving a UPS truck and planning a public relations campaign, when it comes to PR, we are already starting to see the very first drips of automation.

According to one survey of chief marketing officers (CMOs), more than half are already using AI to save time and automate their campaigns. As it stands, 57% of CMOs are using AI to personalise marketing content, another 57% are relying on it to automate customer insights and 50% are using AI-powered software to identify and target new audiences. [37]

While this may sound like small fry stuff when compared to other industries, all of these individual tasks would have previously taken hours, days or even weeks for humans to complete.

Typically, junior members of the team (interns, account executives, etc.) would have been responsible for leading on these tasks from start to finish, being paid to research target audiences, trawl through data, identify potential customer insights and report these insights back to the client. During this process, these junior team members would have consulted third-party research firms, data analysts or even consumer psychologists to build an accurate profile of their customers and campaign audiences.

Now, however, none of these groups needs to be involved.

All of this work can be conducted (at least to a semi-acceptable standard) by a single individual with access to the right AI-powered research and audience profiling tools. These tools call upon a combination of consumer surveys, social media profiles and other big data sets.

The same is true for media relations. 10 years ago, junior PR pros would have learned the ropes by getting to know the press, reading the papers, meeting up with journalists and building their own relationships. Now, there's seemingly little point to these mundane tasks.

Vast media databases built from a combination of friendly journalists sharing their contact info and largely unethical web scraping mean that anyone's details can be found in an instant.

Automated list-building software also means that PR professionals can build highly accurate targeted lists of journalists and influencers, taking into account everything from their interests to their follower counts, their previous articles, and even the key terms they've tweeted about.

Lastly, automated distribution software can provide these PR pros with contact details for each of their highly targeted audiences, blasting out semi-customised pitch emails and press releases en masse. All of this can be done instantly and at the push of a few buttons.

I'm aware I'm starting to sound like a bit of a luddite. Like an old man moaning about the fancy, time-saving technologies that 'you kids have today'. That's not my intention. If new technology can speed up the process of PR and cut out some of the drudgery involved, then that can only be a good thing.

My point, however, is that PR professionals need to recognise these new technologies for what they are — a rapidly encroaching form of automation in an industry that was supposedly immune to such change.

Thanks to these tools, agencies that once would have needed 50–60 staff members can now conduct the same level of work with only 30–40. In future, they could do the same with 10–20.

But it's not just agencies that are starting to adopt such widespread (if somewhat unrecognised) automation. Agency clients and PR professionals working in house are proving to be just as receptive to the lure of automated marketing.

Through AI-powered marketing automation platforms such as Adobe and HubSpot, brands can now run fully-fledged marketing campaigns without any agency support. With an in-house team of only two or three marketers, today's brands can create their own content, run promotions, deliver email marketing campaigns, tailor customer experiences, follow up on purchases, qualify sales leads, tweak product prices and even manage in-store promotions — all from their computer screens. This type of do-it-yourself marketing puts the agency model at a serious disadvantage, pushing it further in the direction of pure-bred consultancy rather than acting as an implementation partner. It also further reduces the need for large agency-side workforces.

Whether marketers recognise it or not, this change is a form of automation. It's also more drips before a ketchup splash waiting to happen.

While the use of AI-powered marketing automation software is now commonplace across the industry, the use of AI in other areas is also growing. According to the latest reports from the Chartered Institute of Public Relations (CIPR), the PR industry is already seeing growing use of AI tools for forecasting, analysis and data management. Within five years, the group expects AI to be much more widely adopted, being used for everything from risk analysis and behavioural analysis to auditing and community identification.[38] And remember, that's according to an industry body managed and run by PR professionals — those rarely best placed to judge the true effects of radical change (see Richard Susskind's previous quote about rabbits guarding the lettuce patch).

Regardless of whether the CIPR's analysis is an accurate or conservative estimate of AI's impact on the industry, this all feels like a lot of change for a profession supposedly 'safe' from automation. If everything from reporting and audience segmentation to behavioural targeting and media relations is being increasingly automated, then what does that leave for the rest of us?

Well, to give you the optimistic answer, it leaves us all the fun stuff. The creativity, consultancy and strategy.

Who really likes reporting? Who wants to spend hours building media lists or segmenting audience data? If those tasks can be automated then we, as professionals, can crack on with doing the stuff that makes PR such a fulfilling profession.

While that's great news for someone who's worked in PR for a long time, we shouldn't pretend that it's good news for the entire industry. As Jim Sterne points out in *AI for Marketing*, when automation comes a-knocking, it's often the younger, junior members of staff (those who undertake the more mundane tasks) who ultimately suffer.[39]

If we automate reporting, traditional pitching, data analysis and PR admin, then the need for an army of interns, juniors and account executives disappears. As Sterne puts it, "we could be very much to a point where the traditional career ladder gets pulled up after us".[40]

Going forward, agencies will not only need to reduce the number of junior staff but will also need to focus on training their staff up to become the next generation of strategic consultants. In some ways, it would be easy to imagine the agency recruitment model being restructured into something closer to that of a pre-internet law firm.

With less grunt work to do, agencies have the opportunity to rebrand as consultancies. Instead of employing 20 account executives to manage day-to-day tasks, they could recruit a handful of apprentices, teaching them how to think strategically, maximise their creative talents, and manage the arsenal of automation software now at their disposal.

6.
Meeting in the middle

While the automation of seemingly mundane tasks may make us feel like we're saving time and becoming more productive, it's worth asking at what cost those savings come. In my last book, *Technoutopia*, I wrote about the fact that every new technology represents both a loss and a gain — something I still firmly believe.

Supposedly, by automating the mundane elements of PR we should be freeing ourselves up to focus on the more intelligent, strategic elements of our work. Sadly, the opposite's true. Since automation platforms entered the workplace, we seem to have less time than ever before to sit around thinking, planning and experimenting with new ideas. Instead of freeing up time, new technologies encourage us to multitask — ticking off more tasks, but rarely devoting ourselves fully to a single piece of work.

Writing in *The Glass Cage: Automation and Us*, American technologist Nicolas Carr explains this phenomenon:

"The danger looming over the creative trades is that designers and artists, dazzled by the computer's superhuman speed, precision, and efficiency, will eventually take it for granted that the automated way is the best way. They'll agree to the trade-offs that software imposes without considering them. They'll rush down the path of least resistance, even though a little resistance, a little friction, might have brought out the best in them."[41]

Personally, I believe that this issue is increasingly facing the PR industry. Being able to do lots of things faster doesn't always translate to doing them well.

Things will be even more complicated for the next generation of PR executives joining the workforce pre-armed with all of these automation and productivity tools.

The automation of everything from building campaign timelines to profiling audiences, building media lists and scheduling email distributions is increasingly seen as normal to these PR pros. Tasks that would have taken a week now take a day, and those that would've taken a day take barely an hour.

By taking such a hasty, overly automated approach, we lose the opportunity for these new executives to build knowledge, to develop expertise and to hone their craft.

Of course, that's not to say we shouldn't use the available tech. If the software's there and it means you can leave by 5pm, then by all means use it. If I was an intern on a starter salary, I'd be doing the exact same thing. My frustration is with the agencies themselves — agencies who are using these technologies to increase workloads rather than to improve results.

Instead of using the time saved to grow and develop their teams, or even to check that the work being automated is the best it can be, a growing number of agencies are stretching their teams across more and more accounts. I've seen agencies piling people with 12 or 15 different client accounts, working them to the point of nervous exhaustion for the sake of additional profits. As the role of automation expands in PR, it should be our responsibility as managers, directors and agency owners to ensure the time saved is being used to improve quality not quantity.

To do that, we need to slow down and take the time to check whether the work being pumped out by our increasingly automated systems is actually of the quality we would expect from a human professional. If it's not, then *there is no time-saving element involved*. Time is only saved if the quality remains unaffected. Perhaps even more importantly, this overreliance on technology means we're at risk of failing to teach the next generation of PR professionals how to do their jobs effectively.

As perhaps the most mundane agency-side example I can think of, let's talk about the process of sending out a press release.

Let's say you want to reach certain audiences and you think the press are the best way to go about it. So, you log in to your media database tool of choice, type in a few keywords to see who writes about your chosen topic and then export those names as a media list. Now you can use your automated release distribution software to start spamming these individuals with press releases.

Thanks to automation, that process was super speedy, perhaps taking less than 30 minutes in total. Even so, those 30 minutes were a complete waste of time.

No insight has been gained. No real understanding of why these people cover the topics they do. No personal relationships have been built or past experiences used. No customisation or personal touches added. No thought given for the ethics involved in essentially spamming complete strangers. No real care for why these tired, overworked and underpaid journalists should give a crap about you, your press release, or your client in the long run.

I'd like to think no PR professional worth their salt would take the automated approach outlined above, and yet I am continually amazed by the number of people (agencies and clients) who seem to think that such an approach constitutes good media relations.

Of course, the alternative is a lot more time consuming. Tailoring stories, building relationships, getting to know a journalist's beat — maybe even getting pissed with them at some tradeshow in Barcelona. That all sounds like a pretty inefficient way of working, but if the end result is disproportionately better, then it's actually more, rather than less efficient.

In summary, automation has taken something complicated that worked and turned it into something simple that doesn't.

And sure, press release distribution is just one tiny corner of this massively varied profession, but this exchange is happening all across the PR industry — especially agency side. Mundane, tactical and seemingly simple tasks are being automated and, in the process, being oversimplified. The result is something far worse for the industry as a whole.

Let's look at another example: audience research.

Why go to the trouble of running surveys and focus groups when you could just pull some audience insights (and I use the word 'insights' lightly) off Twitter and dump them in a

PowerPoint deck? Who needs professional data analysts, ethnographic researchers or trained consumer psychologists when anyone can lift their own conclusions from Google Analytics?

The problem with all of these automated and intuitive tools is that having access to them doesn't make you an expert. If anything, it makes you even more likely to undertake biased research or to jump to incorrect conclusions about your audiences, PR strategy or campaign results.

This isn't just a problem for PR. The ready availability of intuitive, automated analytics software is becoming a real issue for any industry that relies heavily on data analysis. Marketer Jim Sterne explains this problem more succinctly than I ever could, saying:

"As analytics becomes more accepted, demanded and democratised, more and more amateur analysts will be deriving conclusions from raw material they trust implicitly rather than understand thoroughly. Preparing for data-illiterate explorers requires even more rigour than usual to guard against their impulse to jump to the wrong conclusions."[42]

The problem, once again, is that we've convinced ourselves that technology is making us more productive — that our mad rush is a sign of efficiency rather than sloppy workmanship. By encouraging us to trust the output of machines, to not question their findings and to move onto other tasks rather than perfecting what's in front of us, automation runs the risk of making us lazier as employees, as consultants, and as a profession. It's providing the PR industry with free rein to 'rinse and repeat' the same old tactics and to redraw the same conclusions over and over again. Safe, repetitive tactics justified through poor data analysis... the perfect breeding ground for bad PR.

This negative effect is only going to get worse as automated systems become more advanced and AI becomes a more reliable decision maker. In tech communities, it's common to talk about this idea as the 'automation paradox', how increasingly automated systems encourage a lower standard of work, which, eventually, undermines the benefits of automation. As American tech writer Nicholas Carr describes it:

"When a computer takes over a job, the workers are left with little to do. Their attention drifts. Their skills, lacking exercise, atrophy. Then, when the computer fails, the humans flounder. Software designed to eliminate human error ends up making human error more likely."[43]

This atrophy of human skills isn't a theoretical concept; its magnitude has been well documented across numerous industries where automation has already come into play.

As just one example, look at the aviation industry. These days, the vast majority of what a pilot would have once done in the air is now entirely automated. Autopilot systems allow aeroplanes to reach their destinations safely, following a trajectory without the need for constant intervention. In exchange for this automation, those in the aviation industry have become increasingly aware of human pilots 'losing their edge'. In fact, in 2013 the Federal Aviation Administration reported that an overreliance on automation had become a major factor in air disasters. Their advice? Give pilots more of an opportunity to fly manually and transfer some responsibility away from computers and back to people.[44]

A similar effect can be seen in the automotive industry, with companies like Toyota having to recall millions of vehicles with manufacturing defects because of a "loss of human insight and talent."[45]

Technology has a way of encouraging us to only focus on the problems that it's designed to solve. That means that issues like inefficiency suddenly get pushed to the top of our list, while other concerns — things that a computer may not be best placed to help with — get bumped to the back of the queue. It's the law of the instrument: to a man with a hammer, everything looks like a nail.

Of course, PR is nowhere near as automated as the aerospace or automotive industries right now, but the same opportunities for complacency apply.

Returning for a minute to a more mundane example, as anyone who works agency side knows, there's a growing struggle to get PR people talking on the phones or networking at 'real-world' events. Something that was once the staple of public relations — direct human communication — is now dying out.

While there are several reasons for this, the 'law of the instrument' is key among them. Computers can't help you in that scenario. When you're face to face with a random stranger (or over the phone with a reporter you barely know), there's simply no software to rely on and no screen to hide behind.

As an industry we've become masters at hiding behind computer screens. We create digital content, autogenerate media lists, communicate via instant messaging, read alerts from Google Analytics, email our clients and tweet journalists. All of it very important stuff I'm sure, but it's only half the job.

For public relations to work we need to have both virtual and physical interaction. We cannot succumb to only doing half a job purely because that's the half we can do sitting at a computer screen.

The more we sit at our desks, and rely on automated systems, the more likely we are to miss out on new ideas and new ways of working. As PR professionals, it's our job to strive to be better and to try new and more creative ways of doing things. That means opening ourselves up to a variety of experiences (especially those that don't involve sitting at a screen).

This is the irony of our automated future. Our growing reliance on tech means that the AI that could one day replace us won't even need to be that good. As the creative and strategic quality of our work diminishes and we focus solely on repetitive tasks that can be achieved at a screen, we become easier to automate and replace. We are meeting the machines in the middle.

Now, to be fair to creatives working in PR, this is also down to a general professionalisation of the PR industry. To justify its budgets and be taken seriously as a profession, PR has inevitably had to focus on more quantifiable and measurable tasks. To some extent, networking, creativity and the more human elements of the job needed to be sacrificed to make this possible. Spend has to be justified and activities need to fit neatly into the corporate sales funnel — the fluffier and more human the task, the harder that is to do. And I get that.

Professionalisation and automation are both important and, in some ways, inevitable for this industry. But that doesn't mean these things should come at the expense of good creative work. If we're going to survive as an industry — and retain our jobs in the face of automation — we need to get back to basics and focus on the things that made PR so effective in the first place.

When asked what Toyota could do to fix its skills shortage in the face of automation, one executive told *Bloomberg News*, "We need to become more solid and get back to basics, to sharpen our skills and further develop them." The company has since set about replacing some of its robots with skilled workers and craftsmen.[46]

This is exactly what PR — and particularly PR agencies — should do to survive in the age of automation. We must focus on our *craft*, not just our profession. The areas that machines will struggle to replace are twofold: consultancy (strategy and advice) and true creativity (original thought and action). If, like Toyota, we can refocus on these human elements, we may be able to reshape PR for a new era.

Of course, none of this is guaranteed. With the rate at which AI is evolving, the roles that make PR and marketing resilient to automation are never truly going to be 100% safe.

As we'll see in part 2 of this book, nothing is off the table. From creativity to strategy, client relationships and even networking, artificial intelligence projects are already underway that could fundamentally change all elements of PR. That said, I believe that these elements (creativity and consultancy) remain our best bet, offering the 'highest ground' to avoid the coming flood of automation.

PART 2

"The idea that humans will always have a unique ability beyond the reach of non-conscious algorithms is just wishful thinking."

— Yuval Noah Harari, historian and philosopher[47]

7.
The god of the gaps

Whether or not you agree that a profession like PR could be entirely replaced by machines, at this point it should be clear that a serious move towards automation is not entirely off the cards.

PR agencies are not 'safe' by definition. More importantly, any industry that has fallen into the trap of viewing itself as impervious to change has typically been faced with a nasty surprise.

While PR agencies may not be immune to automation, for now at least it seems that machines are doing little more than the mundane day-to-day tasks that practitioners would once have fobbed off on junior staff. Measurement, reporting, admin and time management may be more automated than ever, but it's the human elements of our profession — the creativity, strategy and consultancy — that are supposedly safe from automation.

In reality, artificial intelligence is now evolving at such a pace that it will soon be banging on the door of even the most revered human traits.

Things that only five years ago would have seemed impossible for a machine to replicate are now being trialled in the laboratories of Amazon, Google and Facebook. At the very heart of these experiments is an attempt to crack creativity, strategy and human emotion, all fundamental parts of the PR profession.

When thinking about AI's power to replace these uniquely human characteristics, I'm always reminded of a chapter in Richard Dawkins's The God Delusion, in which he describes the 'god of the gaps'.

The idea, which Dawkins is characteristically angry about, is that religious zealots have a tendency to worship gaps — those phenomena that science cannot yet explain. The view is that God fills these gaps by default, until science eventually uncovers the real explanation. As Dawkins explains:

"Creationists eagerly seek a gap in present-day knowledge or understanding. If an apparent gap is found, it is assumed that god, by default, must fill it. What worries thoughtful theologians... is that gaps shrink as science advances, and god is threatened with eventually having nothing to do and nowhere to hide."[48]

To me, this god-of-the-gaps theory also offers an adequate metaphor for the way that most of us view our own humanity when faced with the growing achievements of artificial intelligence.

We're impressed that AI can master an Atari video game, but we know it will never master something as complex and uniquely human as chess. Five years later, we're impressed that AI has mastered chess, but it will never master something as complex and uniquely human as Go. Five more years later, we're impressed that AI has mastered Go, but it will never master something as complex and uniquely human as driving a car. And so the gaps go on and on and on.

In PR, we have our own unique set of gaps. We tell ourselves that, sure, AI could undertake simple daily tasks like measurement and reporting, but it could never replace us as thought leaders, copywriters, strategists or creative consultants. These are the uniquely human things that make our profession so fluid, innovative, and ultimately human.

In reality, the automation of all of these concepts is already well underway. In the case of copywriting, the reality is already almost upon us. As for AIs offering creative ideas and even strategic advice, many of these algorithms are either in the works or, in some cases, already in use.

Our gaps allow us to protect our egos, to feel that we offer something uniquely human and provide an expertise that no series of 1s and 0s could ever replace.

To return to Daniel and Richard Susskind's point in chapter 5: all professionals think AI would be wonderfully effective at replacing any task in any field... but just not their bit.

If we're to understand the future of our jobs and industry, we need to get over the idea that these gaps are untouchable. Part 2 of this book will consider this idea, examining each of these sacred cows in turn and looking at the hard evidence that they may soon be replaced by algorithms, automation and AI.

While this sounds pessimistic, it doesn't need to be. Once we understand the reality of our future, we can begin preparing for it. And no, that doesn't mean quitting PR and waiting for the robots to take over.

The next 10 years represent a huge opportunity for those PR professionals and agencies looking to trial a new more exciting and more future-proof approach. This is an opportunity to reimagine PR, to revisit our roots as consultants and to rebuild the agency model from the ground up. It's also an opportunity to reconsider what we do, asking what adds the most value and how we can be more effective and even more ethical as an industry.

8.

Anything you can do, AI can do better

Before getting into exactly how automation could come for the sacred cows of PR, it's worth briefly addressing a couple of the great fallacies of AI.

The first is the mistaken belief that intricate, seemingly abstract things cannot be broken down into smaller, more logical steps.

One of the reasons that routine jobs have been so easy to automate is that they follow clear predictable patterns that are easy for a human to define and programme. The fallacy, however, is to assume that such predictability only applies to routine tasks. With enough time and effort, predictable patterns can be found in just about anything — even abstract undertakings such as music and art.

For a good example, check out the work of musicology professor David Cope. A few years ago, Cope built Experiments in Musical Intelligence (EMI), which specialises in imitating the style of Johann Sebastian Bach. It took seven years to create the programme, but once the work was done, EMI composed 5,000 new Bach chorales in a single day.[49]

In my own work, I have helped create and promote a similar AI algorithm, allowing people to generate their own Beatles, Kendrick Lamar and Taylor Swift songs by finding subtle patterns in their lyrical styles.[50]

These patterns are what define so much of our favourite music, reminding us that things that feel intangible and emotional very often follow subtle and repeatable rules.

We know that music performed in a major key sounds happy while a minor key sounds sad.[51] We can also recognise patterns in artists' performance styles, and even identify strict mathematical components in the work of many classical composers.[52] As Cope himself summarises, "I don't know of a single piece of expressive music that wasn't composed, one way or another, by an algorithm."[53]

Thinking about PR, we shouldn't be so arrogant as to assume that what we do can't be broken down into bite-sized chunks, even if it appears abstract or creative on the surface.

Considering this possibility, futurist Martin Ford suggests that a good question to ask yourself is: could another person learn to do my job by studying a detailed record of everything I've done in the past? If the answer is yes, then there's a good chance that AI could learn to do it as well.[54]

Considering my own career, I've been responsible for training countless young PR professionals, often providing them with examples of the things that have and haven't worked for me in my profession. That's how we all train people. By breaking down our own experiences and providing step-by-step guidance, we help teams unlock their own creativity, pose their own ideas and think more strategically about what they do. Looking ahead, I struggle to see any reason why a machine couldn't do the same.

So that's our first AI fallacy — assuming that complex ideas can't be broken down into repeatable patterns and bite-sized tasks.

The second, is the mistaken belief that for a machine to replace a person, it must perform tasks in the exact same way that a human would.

People make this mistake all the time, assuming that AI would need to be so advanced as to replicate the exact thinking processes of a human before being capable of completing a task to the same standard. This is categorically untrue. For most tasks (and even some jobs) machines don't need to comprehend what they're doing, they just need to do it. AI can rarely precisely copy human decisions, but they can perform actions with the exact same outcomes. The best explanation I've found for this distinction comes from Daniel Susskind:

"If you asked Tiger Woods to explain how he hits a golf ball so far, he might be able to offer you insight into a few of the thoughts that pass through his mind as he swings the club. He might also perhaps pass on a few hints. But he would struggle to articulate the complex network of accumulated heuristics, intuitions, and hand-to-eye interactions that have contributed to his supremacy as a golfer. Many of these will be unconscious, learnt through repeated practice and use, and some so deeply embedded that even Tiger himself would be unaware of them. Yet none of this precludes us from building a mechanical swinging arm that could hit the golf ball further and straighter than Tiger."[55]

The same is true for most AI algorithms. Traditional strategic thought did not allow Deep Blue to win at chess —

brute-force processing and an ability to calculate millions of game combinations in a matter of seconds ultimately won the game. Similarly, AlphaGo did not win by playing like a human, it invented new strategies that no human player had ever considered, redefining the conventions of the game to suit its own programmatic approach.[56]

When we consider the aspects of PR being discussed over the next few chapters, it's important to understand that, often, machines don't need to operate at the same complex, conscious, or even emotional level that humans do. Sometimes a "mechanical swinging arm" will do just fine.

9.

Creativity can be coded

If you ask any PR person what they enjoy about their job, the opportunity to act and think creatively will be pretty high up on the list.

Most of what we do is about grabbing attention, and you can't do that by showing people something they've seen a million times before. Creativity, unique stunts and ideas generation are all huge parts of the PR profession.

This focus on creativity is particularly important for those working agency side. A reputation for creative thinking can help agencies stand out from the competition, attract the best employees and bag the top industry awards. Creativity is also essential for landing new clients, with in-house marketers ranking creativity as one of the most important factors when selecting a new agency.[57] Still, despite everyone demanding creative PR, very few people can define what 'creativity' really means, where it originates, or the process behind its formation.

Given this intangible nature, there's a strong argument to say human creativity can't be replaced by machines. Without knowing where it comes from or how it's defined, it's simply too vague of a concept to ever replicate effectively.

While attempts have been made throughout history to build creative machines, many of the world's most famous computer programmers have been forced to draw the same conclusion: creativity cannot be programmed.

Among the most cited examples is Ada Lovelace, the mathematics pioneer and first true computer programmer. According to Lovelace, "The analytical engine has no pretensions whatever to originate anything."[58] Put simply, computers can only operate on what they're given. They cannot think creatively to generate anything truly new.

Several artists and musicians have also considered (and dismissed) the possibility that their creative talents could be broken down and programmed as a series of simplified instructions or rules. Composer Claude Debussy once wrote, "Works of art make rules; rules do not make works of art" while Pablo Picasso declared that the "chief enemy of creativity is good sense".[59] For these creative geniuses, the process of true creativity is not about programmable rules or following a set of instructions, it's about doing things differently, without immediate cause or clearly defined reason. Anything less is no longer a creative act.

While the creativity behind a PR campaign is hardly comparable to the works of Debussy or Picasso (although I'm sure some creative directors like to think so), the process is the same. While many of us run brainstorms and follow a few best practices, there's no one strict formula for generating creative ideas.

In fact, many of the best campaign ideas I've seen have seemingly appeared out of nowhere. Usually it's outside of office hours, in bed, in the shower, or even down the pub that you find creativity suddenly strikes. That moment always feels miraculous, often because it seems so glaringly out of place.

From even these personal experiences, it's clear that creativity cannot be 'programmed' as a traditional, linear piece of software. That said, artificial intelligence isn't any traditional piece of software. AI doesn't need to be programmed — it simply needs a goal to point at.[60]

Already, numerous efforts have been made to build AI capable of creative thoughts and actions — from David Cope's algorithm EMI to projects like Simon Colton's Painting Fool, which paints original artworks in its own unique style.[61] Recent AI projects have also proved extremely effective at generating original storylines and unique ideas — ideas that were never preprogramed or even conceived of by humans.

In one study, researchers built a 'What if' machine (WHIM), with an artificial intelligence component tasked with the goal of generating original storylines for movies and books. At present, WHIM generates short 'what ifs' under five fictional categories: Kafkaesque, alternative scenarios, utopian/dystopian, metaphors and Disney. While the results are still a mixed bag, many of WHIM's suggestions could prove serious money spinners for the film industry, including its idea for a new Disney movie about "a little atom who lost his neutral charge".[62]

Of course, there's a strong argument to say that none of these projects represent true creativity. Most of what's being achieved in the field of artificial intelligence right now represents only 'supervised machine learning', where an algorithm is frequently monitored and recalibrated through ongoing training — often with input from a human overseer.[63] Another criticism is that tools such as David Cope's EMI may well be composing original music, but they're doing so by simply building on the work of human artists, mimicking, editing and restructuring existing styles.

My question would be: does this count as true creativity? And if not, then what does?

The Beatles built on the music of Elvis Presley — who in turn built on the music of Chuck Berry, Fats Domino and a whole host of African American blues and gospel singers. Does that mean that The Beatles's creativity doesn't count? Is something only creative if it's 100% new, with no outside influences or lessons learned from what came before?

This line of questioning can lead you down an extremely deep rabbit hole — one that we thankfully don't need to venture down for the purposes of this book. But, when thinking about creativity from the limited perspective needed to talk about PR, there are really only a few points that are worth exploring.

The first, is the difference between what researchers call 'big-C' creativity and 'little-c' creativity. Big-C refers to those rare acts of creativity that are so novel that they completely change the game.[64] People like Sigmund Freud, Albert Einstein and Pablo Picasso are held up as good examples of big-C thinkers — people whose creative ideas altered the entire fields in which they worked.

Most people, however, will never be big-C creatives. Instead, most of us are little-c creatives. These are people who have the capability to do things in novel ways, without necessarily changing the world (or the rules of their particular field) in the process. This type of thinking is far more applicable to the field of PR, and could potentially prove easier for machines to replicate.

The second concept of creativity worth discussing comes from AI scientist and psychologist Margaret Boden. According to Boden, all creativity falls into one of four camps: exploratory, combination, transformational and psychological.[65]

Exploratory creativity involves taking ideas that already exist and exploring their outer edges, extending the limits of what's possible without breaking the rules of the game. This is where most human creativity is achieved (Boden estimates around 97%).[66]

Returning to our previous example, consider a band like The Beatles. In the 1960s, The Beatles pushed the limits of pop music, creating something entirely new through their own unique sound and performance style. During this time, however, the band didn't escape the confines of the pop genre. They were still playing traditional instruments, following a clear rhythm and producing songs that people could dance to. That is exploratory creativity in action.

Of course, later The Beatles would begin to push their music further, breaking beyond the boundaries of traditional pop music. Through songs like Revolution 9 (a looped sound collage of a man repeating "number nine" over and over) The Beatles broke past exploratory creativity and began to create something entirely new.[67]

The second type of creativity identified by Boden is combination creativity. This involves taking two completely unrelated concepts and combining them into something new. Examples could be the application of mathematics to poetry, psychology to art, or even architectural principles to music. Often, what feels like a stale or overused framework for one discipline can encourage a whole new way of thinking when applied to a separate field. This is still creativity, but it borrows heavily from existing materials, principles and ideas.[68]

Boden's third form of creativity is by far the most abstract: transformational creativity. This is the big-C creativity — those game-changing ideas that revolutionise societies or specific fields.[69] This is by far the hardest form of creativity for computers (or even people) to emulate, but it's also the form of creativity that surfaces the least. For most of us (working in PR or otherwise), true transformational creativity is not something we will ever experience.

The fourth and final form is psychological creativity. This is far more common and often comes down to sustained acts of personal creativity (doing things that are novel to us but not to society as a whole), with the aim of one day producing something that is recognised by others as new and of value.[70]

So that's creativity in a nutshell. The question now is, what type of creativity do we as PR professionals most frequently rely on? Is it the big-C creativity that's proved so hard for machines to replicate? Or is it something far simpler?

Most of us can admit that, while our ideas may be creative, they hardly count as big-C creativity. We're not looking for masterpieces or to achieve something that's never been done before. All we want to do is create something vaguely new, that's surprising enough to grab people's attention, and that will ultimately create value for either our businesses, ourselves or our clients.

Thinking in the terms of Boden's four stages, what PR professionals do doesn't need to be transformational. Typically, it involves pushing the boundaries of what has come before (exploratory creativity) or in the best cases, creates a new approach by learning from other disciplines (combination creativity).

When faced with a challenging creative brief, most of us will turn to what has come before for inspiration.

There's a reason why PR professionals subscribe to inspirational publications like Contagious, Creative Bloq or Famous Campaigns. It's for the same reason that we attend award ceremonies and subscribe to a billion different newsletters — we want to see what creative ideas are already out there so that we can build on them and inspire our own. There's nothing wrong with that, it's just the reality of working in an industry that demands creativity to a strict deadline.

When asked to work in this way, it's no surprise that most PR professionals fall back on exploratory creativity, operating mainly within the peripheries of what has come before. This, however, is exactly the type of creativity that machines are best placed to replicate.

Our creativity cannot (and should not) be transformative, mainly because it must always fit our organisation's objectives or our client's brief. Creative PR isn't about doing something that's never been done before, it's about answering a simple question — how do I create something that's unique enough to be attention grabbing but also achieves a list of pre-set marketing objectives. When posed in this way, PR becomes much more about problem solving than about true creativity, and that's something that AI is actually very good at.

Consider this example. You build a data set containing the details of every award-winning PR campaign ever created. This data set could call upon old entries from various industry awards, along with case studies from across PR Week, Contagious, Famous Campaigns and other PR trade publications. Most of this data is already labelled in terms of the various clients' objectives and how successful the campaign proved in fulfilling them. Using this as a baseline, artificial intelligence could quite easily generate its own ideas — similar to WHIM's movie storylines — that provide maximum impact for the organisation.

Far better than any brainstorm, AI could churn out hundreds of ideas a day with a calculated probability of success against a set list of objectives. Idea generation could even be tied to the current events of the day, using search data and newsfeeds to identify topics and trends that are of interest to the campaign's target audience.

While this may sound like science fiction, the technology required already exists. Movie studios are using AI to devise original plotlines, authors are using it to inspire new novel ideas and scientists are using it to write hypotheses for future research.[71] The technology is here, it just hasn't been applied to PR yet — but it will.

As businesses begin to realise the time- and cost-saving potential of such technologies, we should expect to see creative ideas generation becoming increasingly automated. Like all of these changes, this shift won't happen overnight.

At first, we should expect to see greater augmentation, with human ideas simply being aided by AI. It's easy to imagine a low-cost ideas generator, designed to throw out creative campaign suggestions as prompts for a human brainstorm.

Going forward however, the need for that human element will reduce. As so-called 'dual-brain' AI evolves, computers will not only be capable of generating their own creative ideas, but also of evaluating their worth and discarding those that do not fit the available budget, timeline or brief.

While we may not see human creativity being replaced altogether, as AI advances, the need for a room full of creative human brains will diminish. This may sound dramatic, but we're already seeing it happen in other creative industries.

Take video games for example. Games like No Man's Sky offer players the opportunity to visit millions of different planets, all with their own environments, atmospheres and individual flora and fauna. 10 years ago, it would have taken an entire room of writers, designers and creatives to develop even a handful of such intricate worlds, yet today the entire game is developed by only four coders, with the rest being imagined entirely by AI.[72]

To assume that PR will be any different, or that our own creative ideas are somehow superior to other fields, is to significantly overstate the role that true big-C creativity plays in our day-to-day lives. The creativity that PR relies on follows limited patterns and rules. It builds on what has come before. At its heart, it is exploratory creativity, and as such, can be coded.

10.
Machines that write

According to the recent PRCA census, one in five PR professionals consider copywriting to be a key part of their jobs — placing it higher in importance than events management or even media relations. This figure rises even higher for freelance PRs, who often get lumbered with the bulk of an agency's or a client's copywriting.[73]

For all the talk of glamourous parties, long lunches and celebrity networking events, writing is still the bread and butter of PR. You have to write articles, fact sheets, press releases, media pitches, positioning statements, op-ed pieces, Q&A responses, ad copy, holding statements and even the occasional speech. And that's just the beginning.

Thanks to PR's new obsession with content marketing, most PR pros can also look forward to churning out insights reports, ebooks, research documents, industry guides, video scripts, blog posts and more. Given all this writing, working in PR feels increasingly like being a professional journalist (just without the autonomy or positive societal impact).

Despite this heavy focus on content and copy, it turns out that effective, persuasive writing is a difficult skill to teach.

Low-quality copy is rampant throughout the industry, being a common complaint among both clients and agencies. In one survey, around half of all newly hired college graduates were found to have poor writing skills — a serious concern for an industry that relies so heavily on written communication.[74]

Thankfully, this is a problem that machines are well equipped to solve.

At its most arbitrary level, copywriting is a science. It's a series of grammatical rules and structures that we humans follow to form clear and readable sentences.

When put in these terms, it's not that hard to imagine computers taking over this skill. In many ways, they already have.

Basic spellcheckers and autocorrect algorithms have existed for decades, with computers using clearly defined rules and regulations to correct and improve our copy.

Now, before I get crucified by any literary nerds out there, I'm not saying that good writing only comes down to a set list of grammatical rules or structures. If that was the case, then any of us could study a rulebook and become the next Shakespeare. What I'm saying is that the structural basis of writing is actually quite easy for a machine to follow. What's harder, however, is copywriting as an art and as a creative endeavour. That's what machines have traditionally really struggled with.

It's one thing to be able to follow the rules of grammar, but what about injecting your own emotions or creative ideas? What about crafting your own poetry or prose? To produce truly great writing, a machine would need to adopt emotions, creativity and possibly even consciousness — three exclusively human traits.

Of course, that's not to say that attempts haven't been made. The effort to build emotive writing machines has been around for well over half a century. As early as 1952, pioneering software engineer Christopher Strachey created the first computer-generated love letters using Alan Turing's random number generator on the original Manchester Mark I computer.[75]

For any lovebirds out there, here's a little taster of that early robotic romance:

Duck Duck
You are my little affection:
My beautiful appetite: My eager
hunger. My covetous love lusts
for your infatuation. My yearning
anxiously clings to your fellow
feeling.

Yours eagerly, M. U. C.

Of course, such early examples were simply being generated from a pre-defined list of words and phrases; they weren't truly being 'written' in the human sense of the word.[76]

Strachey's machine could follow the scientific structure of writing, but it couldn't output anything that wasn't previously input by a human being.

Still, Strachey's machine generated effective examples of combinatory literature and successfully showed off a computer's ability to trick humans into an emotional response — not bad for something built before the invention of the microchip.

Throughout the decades, similar writing machines

continued to evolve, with major progress being made in the '80s and '90s. Probably the most impressive of these creations was the Cybernetic Poet, developed by futurist and inventor Ray Kurzweil.

Kurzweil's creation scanned a selection of poems by a particular author before creating a language model of that author's work. This model incorporated computer-based language analysis and mathematical modelling techniques, allowing the machine to write original poems similar in style to the author analysed (similar to what David Cope's EMI did with the music of Bach). Unlike earlier examples, such as Strachey's love letters machine, this was not a case of stitching together pre-approved phrases — this was original poetry, written by a machine.[77]

In the years since Kurzweil's creation, it's hard to describe just how far this technology has come. With the introduction of artificial intelligence, a new wave of companies (led by Google's DeepMind and Elon Musk's OpenAI) has turned computer-generated writing into a practical, and in some ways preferable, alternative to human copywriting.

Where Ray Kurzweil had to devote years (decades even) to developing and training his cybernetic poet, now the same process can be replicated in a matter of weeks. In fact, while working for an AI client at my current agency, I recently helped to train this type of copywriting programme, using it as nothing more than a quick PR stunt.

To coincide with World Shakespeare Day, I worked with my client to launch a tool that could generate new

Shakespearean sonnets at the push of a button. Of course, where this once would have been front-page news, such technology is now so old hat that it was only worth a small mention in a couple of national papers. Clearly, this technology is now commonplace enough to no longer be impressive.

In the last five years we've seen the development of AI poets, lyricists, script writers and even authors. In fact, AI copywriting is now so advanced that programmers have devoted a whole month to the creation of AI-generated novels. National Novel Generation Month, founded in 2013, is a free event encouraging coders to spend November writing code that can generate novels of 50,000 words or more.[78] While the early results varied in quality, more recent years have seen the creation of some truly poignant — if occasionally abstract — literature. I'd highly recommend reading *The Infinite Fight Scene* for a good example of what this technology can produce.

While the quality of these auto-generated novels improves every year, it wasn't until 2020 that the real breakthrough for writing machines took place.

In June 2020, OpenAI launched GPT-3, an 'autoregressive' writing tool described as both the largest and most advanced language model ever created.[79]

Having been fed the entire 52 million-page text of Wikipedia, along with 570 GB of language data pulled from the web, Generative Pre-trained Transformer 3 (GPT-3) can answer questions, draft articles, write essays, summarise long texts, translate languages, take memos, and yes, even write press releases.[80]

To mark the launch of this unprecedented algorithm, *The Guardian* commissioned GPT-3 to write an op-ed piece describing its own conception and explaining its future place in the world (terrifying I know). For those worried about the apocalyptic consequences of AI, this op-ed did little to quell their fears, with GPT-3 immediately declaring:

"I know that I will not be able to avoid destroying humankind. This is because I will be programmed by humans to pursue misguided human goals and humans make mistakes that may cause me to inflict casualties."[81]

Ignoring the genocidal themes, there's no denying that this is a well written piece of technology commentary. In fact, it's probably better than some of the first draft copy I've received from PR professionals in the past. (Harsh, but true.)

So, what does all this mean for creative copywriting and the future of PR?

Well, if you want to see what's going to happen in public relations, then the best thing to do is check out what's already happening in the worlds of advertising and journalism. Within these fields, the introduction of automated copywriting is already well underway.

Where once, ad firms were primarily led by the creation of copy for print ads, today it's social media advertising that receives some of the largest budgets.

Writing copy for a Twitter or LinkedIn ad is totally different to drafting a slogan for a billboard or a newspaper. The contents of traditional adverts are rarely customised, whereas online, one advertising agency can now disseminate up to 10,000 customised ads *per minute*.[82]

The idea of humans drafting copy for all these ads is clearly insane. As such, a growing number of agencies are relying on algorithms to analyse their ads' audiences and then generate personalised copy based on what will be most effective for each individual viewer.

This automation is not only making ads more relevant for people but is also making them more effective, tweaking the copy to improve clickthrough rates. In fact, adverts written by AI have been shown to have a 68% higher clickthrough rate than their human-drafted alternatives.[83] These kinds of results could put human copywriters at serious risk in future.

Still, it's one thing to churn out promoted tweets and catchy slogans, but what about longer-form copy? Could AI really take over the role of a professionally trained copywriter, or even a journalist?

Well, yes and no.

For years now, machines have been writing at least some of our news content — often without us even knowing it. For the most part, this automation has been exclusive to simple stock market stories — typically anything that tracks financial data without requiring too much real analysis or opinion. Newspapers have long since automated this type of reporting, mainly to save some poor journalists from having to churn out such boring, repetitive copy.[84]

As the tech behind this reporting advanced, and new AI players such as Automated Insight and Narrative Science joined the scene, the role of automated journalism expanded, spilling over from financial and business stories and into the sport sections.

Soon, local and even national papers were using AI to automatically convert scores and game highlights into online news stories — even if they hadn't bothered to send a journalist to watch the game.[85]

In 2016, this technology hit the sporting mainstream when *The Washington Post* announced that it would be using a new AI algorithm called Heliograf to report on the Olympics in Rio.[86] Since then, Heliograf has continued to write columns for *The Washington Post*, churning out over 850 articles focused on news, business, sport and now even politics. Other papers have been quick to follow suit, with *Forbes* releasing its own Bertie system, *Bloomberg* launching Cyborg and both *The Guardian* and *MSN* releasing their own AI journalists (presumably with equally silly names).

In fact, in a recent *Reuters* report, nearly three quarters of media outlets said they are now using artificial intelligence for at least some of their news copy.[87] As the technology behind GPT-3 evolves, we should expect to see such automated journalism becoming increasingly advanced, moving beyond simple 'news' reporting to include long-form opinion pieces, reviews and even satire.

So, what does all this mean for the copywriting elements of public relations, and the numerous copywriters working inside PR agencies?

Well, when it comes to the most formulaic elements of writing, we should expect to see automation advancing rapidly in the next few years.

The whole point of press releases and media briefing

documents is that they follow a set format that journalists can lift a story from. This is exactly the type of content that AI platforms are proving so effective at reproducing. Provided with the key highlights of a story along with a handful of core messages to put across, an AI algorithm could easily generate an effective press release.

In fact, working with Wildfire labs — the marketing division of the agency I work for — one account executive did just that. In the space of only a few weeks, she built and trialled an automated press release writing tool, using the TensorFlow machine learning platform.[88] If this type of tool were combined with the technology described in previous chapters, AI could even be used to generate the idea for a news story and then instantly write a press release to promote it. In this scenario there would be little need for human interaction at all.

The same logic applies to briefing documents and reporting. Clients and spokespeople regularly ask for these briefing docs so that they can brush up on a reporter before an interview. Essentially, they consist of a handful of key facts (typically researched on the internet) about the reporter and publication, a summary of potential questions and a list of the key messages that need to come across during the interview. Once again, it's easy to imagine an AI program that would be capable of trawling the internet (and any prior journalist communications) for this information, before packaging it up in the most digestible format possible for the client.

More directly promotional content; such as copy for

landing pages, websites, product spec sheets and brochures; would also be easy to automatically produce. As long as the machine was provided with a goal and a list of key features or benefits, AI could easily produce compelling copy that drives clickthroughs, downloads and purchases. In fact, several web hosting services are already experimenting with AI tools to do just that.[89]

So that's press releases over with (thank god), but what about the trickier side of PR copy — the articles, opinion pieces and thought leadership?

True thought leadership is going to be a hard thing to replace. Brilliant, inventive people conveying their thoughts, opinions and ideas for the future is not an easy concept for AI to replicate. Thankfully however, most of what counts as thought leadership doesn't come close to this level of originality. With ever stricter deadlines and ever-more content marketing to churn out, much of what passes for thought leadership these days is little more than regurgitated ideas posing as thinly veiled advertorial.

This might sound cynical, but far too often it's the truth. Just take a look through the contributor pages of *Forbes* or any other website that still accepts corporate article submissions. Nine out of 10 articles are just repeating existing ideas, having typically been ghost written by freelancers or PR pros rather than the genuine experts to whom they're attributed.

This type of low-quality content takes me back to the point raised in part 1 of this book — that such low-quality work is making PR professionals easier to automate out of existence.

By over relying on content rehashed from the internet and claiming that it represents real thought leadership we are meeting the machines halfway. We are making ourselves more dispensable.

The point of thought leadership was once to provide journalists with unique, compelling content that both benefited them (by giving their audience something worthwhile to read) and us (by positioning our client or organisation as interesting enough to be worth reading about).

In a market now saturated with poorly formed opinions and low-quality ghost-written copy, it's worth asking whether journalists should even take such content from PRs anymore? When interesting opinions can be generated at the push of a button and then converted into a 1,000-word auto-written article, why bother publishing content hashed together by freelancers and PRs?

Such thinking also poses a real conundrum for PR agencies. Clients rely on agencies to write this type of thought leadership content because they rarely have time to do it themselves. Typically, an agency (or freelancer) will be given a broad topic that a client wants to write about, hold a quick phone call to flesh out their ideas, and then spend a few days researching those ideas online, expanding them and converting them into a fully-fledged thought leadership article. Looking to the future, there's no reason this process couldn't be incorporated into the client's marketing automation platform. By providing AI with a list of concepts and key themes, clients could literally generate their own thought leadership articles for placement — either in the press or on their company blogs.

While this technology does not yet exist (GPT-3 remains largely experimental rather than a product for sale) we should expect to see such products on the not-too-distant horizon. Marketing technology brands such as SAP and Adobe are constantly investing in new ways to automate and streamline marketing, and as tools like GPT-3 evolve, copywriting will be squarely in the firing line.

If PR agencies are to keep their current content marketing remits, then the quality of their content has to improve. The next few years will see an arms race between copywriters and AI, with the production of more exciting, more interesting and more informative content being the weapon at hand. Given the current standards of corporate writing, it seems inevitable that PRs will lose this race, but if we can focus our effort less on churn and more on creating and promoting genuinely interesting ideas, then there may still be a place for copywriting in the future of our profession.

11.

Robot relations: clients and the media

Here it is. The big one: relationships.

We've now seen that machines can write half-decent copy, analyse news angles and even generate their own creative campaign ideas. But what's the point of any of this if they can't sell those ideas to clients or promote their content to the media? PR is all about relationships, but can we still build anything resembling a meaningful relationship if the human elements of our jobs are replaced by machines?

In the short term, this seems like a major stumbling block for the automation of PR. Whether it's online chatbots or menu-based assistants on the phone, people have traditionally hated dealing with automated systems. Given this fact, it's hard to imagine a journalist, or even an agency client, being happy to communicate with a faceless machine rather than building a genuine relationship with a human.

Of course, in the case of journalism, this problem may eventually resolve itself. Automation is only a problem when only *one side* of the conversation has been replaced by a machine, but when both parties have been replaced, the need for human relationships disappears.

Think about it. Chatbots and automated phone calls are only annoying because we humans have to deal with them. But if both the sender and the receiver are automated, then the problem disappears. Applying that same logic to the world of media relations, if ever-more journalists are being replaced by machines, then the idea of PR also becoming more automated becomes less of an issue.

To bring this idea to life, let's take a quick detour to talk about Google Duplex. Launched in 2018, Duplex is an AI assistant, programmed to speak in a convincing human tone. Using this tone, the handy AI is able to phone up restaurants and hairdressers and make bookings on your behalf — all without the person answering even knowing they're talking to a machine.[90] Here's a transcript of one of Duplex's first calls:

> Hairdresser's assistant: "Hello how may I help you?"
> Google Duplex: "Hi, I'm calling to book a woman's haircut for a client... Umm, I'm looking for something on May 3rd?"
> Hairdresser's assistant: "Sure, give me one second."
> Google Duplex: "Mm-hmm."

By relying on human language patterns, including natural pauses and holding phrases like 'umm', Google Duplex successfully tricked the person it was speaking to into believing that it was a real human looking to book a haircut. Clearly, this is incredible technology, but to my mind it raises an obvious question — what's the point?

As this technology rolls out and reduces in cost, surely hairdressers will also look to replace their own assistants with Google Duplex? The same goes for those who typically answer the phones in stores, take deliveries or who book tables in restaurants. Once both the person booking the haircut *and* the person taking the booking have been replaced by automation, then all the 'umms' and 'hmms' become redundant. Google Duplex itself becomes redundant.

Why bother with the cost of a phone call when both sides are machines? At this point, it will be far easier to just tell Google Duplex that you need a haircut, have it look up what's available, and then book in for the closest available timeslot. Suddenly, we're back where we started — an online booking system linked to your calendar.

When thinking about the automation of media relations, we're faced with a similar situation. Right now, no journalist wants to hear from an automated PR, but, as ever-more journalists are automated out of existence, the problem starts to disappear.

In recent years, newsrooms around the world have haemorrhaged staff, looking to replace costly humans with increasingly automated systems. Only last year, Microsoft replaced dozens of contract journalists on its *MSN* platform with algorithmically generated and selected news.[91] Similarly, sites like *The Huffington Post* and *BuzzFeed* have also laid off hundreds of staff, in part driven by the rise of automation.[92]

And that's just the more popular digital brands. Print newspapers have had to be far more aggressive in culling their human workforces. Over the last decade, employment at American newsrooms has fallen by half, with a third of the nation's largest newspapers reporting layoffs since 2017.[93]

This trend has also been replicated in the UK, with *News UK* (owner of *The Times, The Sunday Times, The Sun, VirginRadio* and *talkSPORT*) being forced to announce major job cuts in recent years.[94]

Going forward, newsrooms are set to rely on an ever-smaller number of staff, with algorithms taking over the tasks of researching articles, deciding the top stories and even organising the best layouts for the news.

As automated copywriters and programs like GPT-3 advance over the next 10 years, we should also expect to see robot journalism expand into other more mainstream areas of reporting.

All this will mean big changes for the PR industry. Nobody can schmooze an algorithm, no matter how many drinks you buy it or how many times you invite it to the Christmas party.

As the priority of stories is decided by machines, such biases will (theoretically) be removed.

Without human journalists to make editorial decisions, stories will be ranked based on data, with algorithms identifying the topics and themes that are proving the most relevant, popular or click-worthy, and then tailoring articles to fit those themes.

At the same time, we should also expect the media to become more personalised. As traditional news outlets struggle to compete against social media, many will look to personalise their feeds and even their content to match audience demands.

While I could bang on for hours about the negative, ethical

implications of these changes, that's not really the purpose of this book. What is worth saying, though, is that all these changes will make it harder than ever for human journalists to keep up. The more that news reporting becomes something instant, automated and personalised, the less room there will be for human reporters — and, in turn, less room for PRs to work with them.

Of course, this isn't to say that PRs won't find new and creative ways to inject our clients and ideas into this system (being the wily creatures that we are), but I can't imagine this task will involve much face-to-face networking or human relationship building.

As journalists are automated out of existence, those who remain will be busier than ever.[95] Instead of saving journalists time, the current state of quasi-automation may actually be making their jobs harder. Deadlines are becoming tighter, workloads are becoming more varied, and journalists are increasingly expected to pick up the numerous small tasks that can't yet be automated. During this transition period, the idea of spending time networking with PRs seems even less realistic.

Already, PR professionals outnumber journalists six to one.[96] As such, the idea of journalists maintaining real, meaningful relationships with all these PRs simply isn't feasible. The ever-smaller pool of remaining journalists don't have time to be schmoozed or taken out for long lunches to discuss your agency's client portfolio. Even if they did, they'd still struggle to remember your name in among all the hundreds of PRs who flood their inboxes every day.

This problem is also being added to by the fact that PRs are getting lazier with their own media outreach. As discussed earlier in this book, PR agencies are increasingly relying on pre-built media databases, which combine journalist contact details with information about their newsbeats, areas of interest and pitching preferences. Automated distribution software also allows PRs to blast out quasi-personalised pitches and press releases to these journalists en masse, all without having to get to know who they're actually pitching to.

Now, none of this is to say that I endorse this sort of lazy automated media relations. But there's no denying that it is happening. As these tools become more sophisticated, and journalism itself becomes more automated, the role of face-to-face networking and traditional media relations will inevitably become less and less relevant.

Of course, journalists and influencers aren't the only people that PR agencies have to keep on side. A huge part of agency life is also the relationships that are built with clients.

The good news here is that client relations shouldn't be going anywhere any time soon. Clients love having an agency to rely on. Agencies help clients manage their workloads, measure their results and provide an outsider's perspective to help generate new creative ideas. Best of all, agencies also provide someone to blame whenever the shit hits the fan. (Sorry agencies.)

Still, it's not all about credit and blame. PR agencies are also there to provide their clients with consultancy and a decent 'sounding board' for their own ideas.

It may sound silly but working in house can be quite lonely. I've had many friends move to in-house roles, looking forward to the independence and autonomy involved in 'running the show', only to find that they miss the collaboration and camaraderie of agency life.

Unless you end up working in a giant firm that can justify the cost of an entire marketing department, many in-house PR pros find themselves working largely on their own.

In some ways, this is a blessing. Working alone is a great way to build intelligent plans, conduct research and develop a well-informed strategy. On the creative side, however, things are a lot harder.

While we've all had the occasional spark of creativity while completely alone, often it takes a room full of minds to bounce ideas around. People can help to not only offer new perspectives, but to also pick holes in our existing ideas — or to build on them and convert them into something even better. That type of creative collaborative feedback can be hard to find internally at a business, and it's one of the reasons why so many in-house PR professionals ultimately end up hiring a PR agency.

Now, here's the problem. PR agencies aren't cheap. It's all well and good having a team to help out, or even just to bounce ideas off of — but when that team costs you upwards of £200,000 a year, it's hard not to wonder whether it's really worth it.

To address this concern, PR agencies look to add as much value as possible via an increasingly exhaustive list of services.

Today, agencies offer everything from strategic consultancy

to analyst relations, social media management, and even graphic design, all to justify their fees. By offering these additional services, many agencies hope to make up for the loss of their 'little black books' (the exclusive list of media contacts that they used to hold dear but can now be found by anyone with access to Google).

The perfect example of this was the expansion into so-called 'digital PR' services in the mid-2000s.

Recognising digital marketing as a potential new 'little black book', PR agencies gleefully jumped on the opportunity to offer digital services including pay-per-click advertising, search optimisation and social media management. All of these required seemingly complex and technical skills that clients couldn't yet do in house.

Of course, we now all know that social media requires very little additional expertise beyond the principles of traditional marketing and PR. The same persuasive techniques, focus on strategy, and tried-and-tested 'four Ps' all still apply to good marketing. All that really changed were the tools being used to implement them.

At the same time, these tools have also been increasingly dumbed down to maximise their advertising appeal, reaching a point where literally anyone can use them. Social media marketing is now just as accessible to a mum running a bake sale as it is to a multibillion-pound pharmaceutical company. As such, the magic and mystery that once surrounded digital marketing has worn off.

This growing accessibility is becoming a real problem for PR agencies looking to uncover a new little black book (and justify their significant fees).

Across the board, new, and increasingly automated technologies have made various parts of the PR (and marketing) role easier to do. With a few clicks and the right templates, clients can now launch their own email marketing campaigns, design their own adverts, create and manage their own websites, build their own infographics, monitor their own media coverage, run their own social media profiles, and yes — even distribute their own press releases.

Where once, the tools needed to do all these things were complex and clunky, now a combination of intuitive drag-and-drop interfaces and AI-generated custom templates makes the whole process unbelievably easy.

Provided with these tools, it's becoming ever harder to justify splashing out on creative agencies.

Instead of forking out hundreds of thousands of pounds for a large corporate agency (to receive only a slither of their attention) many clients are now looking to develop their own extremely effective in-house teams.

With the right tools and automation in place, a team of only four or five people can now manage all of a company's marketing, digital, content, PR and advertising campaigns. In many cases, these individuals don't even need to be highly trained (or highly paid) experts.

A small, passionate group, with the right strategy in place, can often be just as effective as a full-service agency. And best of all, they only work for one client! No more divided attentions or sharing your team with 14 or 15 other companies.

Even among my own clients, many are now paying for in-house social and media monitoring tools. And why wouldn't they? The technology is getting cheaper, the tools are becoming easier to use, and the results are getting more accurate every day. Why rely on an agency when you can so easily do all this stuff yourself?

Of course, not everything that a PR or marketing agency does can currently be brought in house. Sure, clients may be able to monitor their own coverage, source their own media opportunities and even distribute their own press releases, but do they really want to spend four hours of their time following up with journalists on the phone?

Perhaps, in future this is where tools like Google Duplex will come into their own, being used to automate this type of labour-intensive personal work. Or, as we've already discussed, it won't even be necessary. As journalism becomes more automated, it's likely that those personal follow ups will become obsolete, offering yet another reason for clients to take their PR activities in house.

It's also worth considering whether paying an agency for media relations will still be worthwhile when so many media outlets are switching to a business model based around advertorial.

Years ago, if you wanted to get your CEO's think piece in a prestigious publication like *Forbes*, the only way to do it was to hire a decent-quality PR agency. That agency would pitch the idea into *Forbes*, and then spend weeks negotiating with the magazine's features editor to ensure that the piece was the right fit for the publication. Next, the agency's team of copywriters would work with the CEO to prepare her article, making sure that it incorporates all of the company's messaging, while still toeing the editorial line strictly enforced by *Forbes*. After several weeks of careful crafting, the agency would submit the CEO's piece, only to have it torn apart by the editor, or bumped from the magazine because of lack of space. Going back to the drawing board, the agency would then alter the focus of the feature and attempt to re-pitch it for the following month's issue. All of this took time, manpower and, ultimately, money, with monthly agency fees quickly racking up in the process.

Now let's look at that same process today. *Forbes* is predominantly read online, with only 6 million readers for its print magazine versus almost 140 million for its digital channels.

To get your CEO's think piece in front of those 140 million people, you phone up the *Forbes* advertorial department and ask to set up a profile on the site. *Forbes* will then ask for your credit card details over the phone and charge you a little under £2,000 to set up a thought leadership profile under your CEO's name.[97] This profile will not only allow your CEO to publish her think piece with only minor editorial edits but will also allow her to contribute ongoing monthly think pieces for the rest of the year. That's it. You're done. 12 articles published in *Forbes*, all with no fuss, no pitching and no expensive agency fees. Your CEO's thoughts are still getting out there and your company name is still appearing in one of the most prestigious business sites on the internet. You can even include links back to your company's website within the article — all with no extra charge. Hell, in the case of *Forbes*, the articles don't even have to be labelled as advertorial, they just include a small note (written in light grey text on a white background) confessing that the author is a 'fee-based' *Forbes* member.

In this strange new world of pay-to-play journalism, it's harder than ever to justify the role of PR agencies selling traditional media relations.

The new acceptability of advertorial, combined with the rise of robot journalism and the introduction of in-house marketing automation tools has PR agencies trapped in a pincer movement. The need for media relationships — or even just media relations — is set to dramatically diminish.

In turn, while relationships with clients will remain just as important as ever, it will be hard for clients to justify keeping their agencies on at such high fees.

A combination of intuitive automation platforms, small in-house teams and a handful of low-cost gig-economy copywriters (at least until GPT-3 gets off the ground) will be more than adequate to replace most agencies.

PART 3

"The readiness with which we accept the notion of our own obsolescence says a lot about how much we value ourselves."

— Douglas Rushkoff, tech writer and filmmaker[98]

12.
Surviving the robot revolution

Throughout this book, we've covered society's long history of underestimating machines. We've seen how technologies that were once considered within the realms of science fiction have come to be accepted as part and parcel of our daily lives.

We've also seen just how quickly those changes can come, with the so-called 'ketchup effect' becoming a common trend for technology adoption. In applying this trend to PR, we've considered how agency professionals have exaggerated both the importance of creative thinking within their daily lives and the uniqueness of their ideas.

We've also seen behind the curtain of creative thought, coming to understand creativity not as some inimitable human trait, but as a process that could one day be artificially replicated.

Finally, we've reviewed the state of creative AI today, examining a new wave of algorithms encroaching on writing, media relations and ideas generation.

So where is this going? Will the next 10 years see all these things becoming entirely automated? Will the need for PR agencies vanish and the world's 3 million PR professionals be out on the street?

Personally, I don't believe that the PR agency will

disappear completely — but I do think that the agency model will need to reshape dramatically in the face of growing automation.

Looking ahead, the agency workforce will begin to shrink, with far fewer people needed to manage the writing, reporting and pitching tasks associated with a traditional agency. The pyramid agency structure will begin to thin at the bottom, with clients requiring agencies for their experience and expertise, rather than their army of junior 'doers'.

Next, the new wave of PR automation tools will make in-house PR professionals (agency clients) far more capable of managing their own projects and campaigns, all with smaller budgets and a far smaller internal team.

Already, many clients are investing in their own PR monitoring and reporting tools — tools which used to be exclusively owned and managed by their agencies. Previously, these tools were expensive and time consuming to use, but as they've grown cheaper and more automated, it's become far easier for clients to justify bringing them in house.

As more and more elements of public relations are automated, we should expect to see this trend expanding. It shouldn't be long before a PR dashboard is added to clients' existing marketing automation suites, encompassing various functions that once would have been undertaken by a team of agency-side professionals.

Functions on this dashboard could include a strategic planning tool, using natural language processing to help convert vague communications objectives into targeted, measurable SMART objectives. This tool could even suggest the best strategies for fulfilling those objectives, calling upon mountains of media, audience and sales data to identify the best methods for segmentation and targeting. It could also export that strategy into a perfectly formatted template, ready to present to the chief marketing officer or the company's board.

And it's not just strategy that would be incorporated into this dashboard. As deep learning technology evolves it may be just as easy to incorporate a creative brainstorming function.

Rather than simply throwing out random ideas, this feature would draw on the agreed strategy, generating a list of creative tactics based on the SMART objectives already set. By checking these ideas against a database of case studies and award entries — not to mention every other campaign executed via the platform — the AI would even assign a likelihood of success score for each tactic produced.

Alongside these high-level tools, more tactical tasks could also be incorporated into the dashboard. With small advances in natural language processing, the age-old process of interviewing a client and then converting their ideas into articles, quotes and blog posts can finally come to an end.

By simply calling on recorded video interviews, AI could easily turn the key points into carefully crafted copy, matching the format, wordcount and tone needed for an editorial or advertorial post. It would even be possible to expand these articles automatically, scouring the internet for supporting data and additional sources to reinforce the spokesperson's key arguments.

Best of all, agencies would not even be needed to place these articles. As journalism becomes more automated and the role of advertorial expands, PR automation tools could start to incorporate automated bidding for paid placements.

Expanding on the model used by Google Ads, in-house PR professionals could literally auto-draft an article in the style needed by a leading publication, review it, set a maximum budget for placement, and then have the article appear as advertorial online the next day. No pitching. No fuss. No agency fees.

For news outlets, and those who don't take advertorial content, media relations software would also be incorporated. Rather than simply blasting out releases (as is so common with current PR distribution software) these tools could take a handful of bullet points provided by the client and convert them into a fully formed press release.

This auto-drafted and heavily personalised release would then be automatically distributed to a list of the most relevant journalists and influencers, all automatically selected based on their previous articles, news beats and an analysis of their social media interests.

I'm aware that when these things are pulled together into a single (albeit imaginary) platform, it sounds like science fiction, but all the component parts are already well underway.

This type of automation may not remove the need for PR agencies altogether, but it does reduce their role, their value and the way that they must be structured... not to mention the prices they charge.

For all their talk of creativity, most PR agencies currently sell their services as a resource — as an army of extra hands that clients can call upon to help manage their workloads and 'get shit done'.

In future, this approach won't be good enough. Who needs an army of copywriters when 80% of copywriting can be generated automatically? Who needs an agency full of interns to manage measurement, media monitoring and reporting when clients can do all of this in house? And who needs media relations experts when an algorithm can analyse everything that's ever been written on a topic and instantly pitch the most relevant stories?

These are all major parts of the current agency model — parts which could all be fundamentally replaceable within the next decade.

So, what should we take away from all this? Should we give up and retrain? Should we quit our agency roles and start fighting for positions in house? Should those currently studying public relations at university drop out and start a proper degree?

How should agencies restructure and how should teams retrain? What happens to the agency model?

How can PR survive the robot revolution?

13.
A new agency model — five steps for survival

I wasn't sure what to call this chapter. In the first draft it was listed as *'Five steps to fighting back'*, which had some nice alliteration, but didn't quite match the sentiment I need to impart.

This isn't a war against machines, and we don't need to 'fight back'. Automation is just a new evolution in the landscape, an evolution to which PR agencies will need to adapt.

As discussed in the last chapter, PR agencies as a whole aren't going to disappear any time soon, but I do think they will change dramatically in the face of growing automation.

Many of these changes have already been introduced (automated reporting, measurement and research), others are just around the corner (automated copywriting, brainstorming and journalism), and some are still only just appearing on the horizon (automated strategy, planning and decision making).

If agencies want to adapt to these changes. then they need to start thinking about the things that will be most valuable when this future arrives.

What are the skills, tools and services that will prove most beneficial after automation takes hold? What are the areas where we can still add value to our clients and their brands?

These are the questions that agency owners and directors will need to start asking if they want to protect their businesses.

Right now, the biggest thing playing in agencies' favours is the fact that clients are extremely time poor. Even with the introduction of new automation and productivity tools, this fact doesn't seem to be changing. The world is getting faster, but it's also getting busier.

The idea that automation would free us up to enjoy endless leisure time was, sadly, a myth. No matter how much work is automated, clients and in-house teams will still be rushed off their feet, and they'll still need agencies to help them navigate the road ahead of them. Agencies will always be able to sell their time, but it's *what that time translates to* that will have to evolve in several ways. With that in mind, these are the five steps to survival that I believe will benefit any PR agency in the face of the coming automation.

1. Sell strategy over tactics

Based on everything discussed throughout this book, it's clear that PR strategy will be one of the last skillsets to be replaced by machines. Machines can write, report, analyse data and aid in creative decision making, but they cannot put together a good strategy.

Both big data and AI will give us a wealth of new resources to help build these strategies, but right now brands still need humans to bring all of those insights together into one clear, coherent vision.

Ensuring your whole agency thinks and acts in a strategic

way will soon be the most vital resource you can offer.

That means taking a step back from the day-to-day. Rather than trying to add yet more products and services to their arsenals, agencies must rebrand their roles with a focus on strategic consultancy. In an age where machines can do the 'doing', it's the thinking that humans will be most needed for. Forget churning out hundreds of press releases and having an army of interns, in an age when menial day-to-day tasks have been automated, the size of your team won't matter. It'll be brains, not brawn that clients value, and they'll be willing to pay to get it.

Of course, in the long term, even strategy may be under siege from AI. Already, IBM's Watson has been used as the basis of a new 'c-suite adviser', scanning thousands of strategy documents and digesting conversations at meetings to provide basic strategic advice for financial institutions.[99]

Still, this type of technology is a long way behind those described in the rest of this book, with few humans truly trusting AI to make strategic decisions for their companies.

For the medium term at least, agencies should feel safe in the knowledge that the more they focus their teams on working with clients to develop messaging and strategy, the more able they will be to add value in the age of automation.

2. Skill up on your successor

Whenever a new automation tool hits the market, there's typically a period of time where agencies adopt it before their clients do. This is often because such tools are initially expensive, and agencies can distribute the cost across multiple client accounts. It's also because clients are both budget conscious and time poor, meaning they don't always get the opportunity to explore every exciting new tool that hits the market. Over time, this changes. Tools become less expensive and more accessible. In some cases, they even become a fundamental necessity that clients simply couldn't live without.

Just look at Google Analytics. Only 10 years ago, agencies fully managed their clients' Google Analytics accounts, but now most agencies struggle to get their clients to even hand over their analytics passwords. Google's technology has become clearer, more automated and more accessible, ultimately to a point where it moved in house and the agency's involvement became obsolete.

The same is now happening with pay-per-click platforms, monitoring tools and even press release distribution software.

Agencies get a golden period of about five years before the magic of these exciting new platforms wears off, and clients begin to realise that they can manage them themselves. This is the period when they can add the most value, helping clients benefit from the latest tools and technologies, without having to spend time and money bringing them in house.

Agencies should make the most out of this period, ensuring that they are up to speed with the latest automated tools — even those that may one day replace them. Staying ahead of this curve is an easy way to ensure that your agency is still adding value.

3. Seek out big-picture skills

With workforces set to shrink and far fewer 'doers' needed in your typical agency, hiring the right staff will be essential.

One of the biggest traps that agencies fall into is hiring people with tactical skills, especially when it comes to the digital world.

I remember a time about five years ago where every agency was tripping over itself to hire people with coding skills. Before that it was SEO, and before that it was 'digital PR' (whatever the hell that is). The problem with hiring people based on these sorts of technology-oriented skills is that they date incredibly quickly.

Just look at my own career. I came out of university having learned ActionScript (a programming language that no longer exists), Adobe Fireworks (a design tool that no longer exists) and experience using several analytics and PR monitoring tools (all of which no longer exist). Staff who are trained in tactics and tools aren't valuable in the long term, especially when it comes to protecting against future automation.

While it may sound contradictory to my advice in step 2, agency staff shouldn't be hired because they know about a particular piece of software or automation tool. They should be hired because they possess the fundamental curiosity needed to learn about that tool — or any future tools that may arise.

This is what I mean by staff with big-picture skills. We need people with curiosity, those who are eager to learn and able to adapt. That also means people who are capable of joining the dots in a strategy and proposing something from a new or interesting perspective.

A second much needed big-picture skill is confidence — with the ability to present, persuade, and articulate ideas that take others along on a journey.

These are the types of skills that make for budding strategists and consultants — not coding, or SEO, or knowledge of some particular media monitoring platform. And yes, this type of skillset is far harder to find in junior employees, but that, again, is where the agency model needs to change.

As the workforce shrinks, agencies will need to hire fewer staff, devoting more time and energy to evolving them in the manner of an apprenticeship. In this new environment, it will be essential to hire staff who show the fledgling signs of curiosity, confidence and strategic thinking — even if it's in the very earliest stages. Then, it will be the vital job of agencies not to overload these individuals with menial tasks, but instead to help turn them into the reliable consultants that clients will so desperately need in future.

4. Be consultants and sell your knowledge

Now is the time, more than ever before, for agencies to restructure themselves around the notion of consultancy. When the 'doing' can be done by machines, the thinking will be more valuable than ever. Knowledge and expertise will always be more valuable than the ability to churn out press releases.

At the same time, as the wealth of data produced by machines explodes, clients will need teams to help them make sense of what they're seeing and to provide guidance based on years of experience. This will be especially essential in the years to come, when algorithmic decision making is increasing but trust is yet to be fully placed in the result. In this messy landscape, businesses will need trusted advisors more than ever.

Currently, agency-side professionals tend to think in terms of campaigns. We do the campaign, and we leave. Or even more common, we propose the campaign and if the client's too stupid to listen then that's their problem.

That's not consultancy.

Great consultancy has to leave ego at the door. It has to take people on a journey, teach them to trust the advice given, and then equip them with the tools to expand on that advice in future. Too few PR agencies do that right now, but in future, it will be the skill that's most needed.

5. Act responsibly

Ok, so I know this one sounds a bit vague, but it's basically because I didn't want to end this book on the phrase "try not to be dicks".

If PR agencies are going to survive and thrive in the age of automation, then we have a duty to act responsibly.

Everyone who works in PR has horror stories, and we've all witnessed some pretty crappy things at bad agencies. Most PRs deal with companies promoting unhealthy products as healthy, clients fudging metrics, people lying about results, campaigns not backed by research or backed up by measurement, stolen ideas, faked statistics, rigged competitions, and enough bullshit to bury the world and everyone in it.

For all the nonsense written about ethics in PR, the truth is that very few of us on the shop floor have time to think about ethics, or to involve ourselves in lofty conversations about industry standards and regulations. And that's a real problem.

I've been very lucky in my career to work with several agencies who do take ethics seriously. More than once at Wildfire (my current agency) we've turned down a high-paying brief because it didn't fit our agency values. That's lovely. Good for us. But that's not the norm.

There are a lot of unethical businesses out there, some with pretty deep pockets, which a lot of PR agencies are happy to chase. But it's not just about working for unethical people, it's about working in an unethical way. You don't have to represent a dictator to be acting unethically (although there are plenty of PR firms willing to do just that).

Often, it's the day-to-day stuff that's really letting the industry down. It's the subtle decisions that fly under the radar. It's people playing to stereotypes, writing clickbait or misleading customers into bad decisions. That's the stuff we need to watch.

Now, thanks to AI, this situation is about to get a whole lot worse.

The thing about automation is that it rarely leads to new ways of working. Instead, it tends to codify existing practices, focusing on increasing the efficiency of the old, rather than implementing the new. This is bad news, as often the only thing worse than bad practice, is highly efficient bad practice.

If PR is ever going to be automated — and believe me, it will — then we cannot risk codifying our own shoddy practices into its design. We must clean up our act and ensure that whatever is automated is designed with ethical use at its heart.

If our role as PR people is to badger and annoy journalists, then that's exactly what our automation tools will do. If it's to churn out low-quality copy and clickbait, then that's also what they'll do. If our job is simply to generate wacky ideas that will win creativity awards but not add any value to our clients' bottom lines then — you guessed it — that's exactly what our tools will do.

As well as these ethical implications, our own low standards are also what are helping speed up the decline of PR in general. The more repetitive, uninspiring and menial the ideas and work we produce is, the easier it is for machines to replicate.

That's why it's on us, as an industry, to be better. To be smart, bold and strategic. To be interested and interesting. To be curious and creative. To be confident and courageous. But most important of all, to try not to be dicks.

Notes

1.   Carufel, R. (2019). *The most stressful jobs of 2019 — "PR Executive" ranked among Top 10.* [online] Agility. Available at: https://www.agilitypr.com/pr-news/public-relations/the-most-stressful-jobs-of-2019-pr-executive-ranked-among-top-10/.

2.   IBM (n.d.). *What is automation?* [online] IBM. Available at: https://www.ibm.com/topics/automation.

3.   Wikipedia Contributors (2019). *Algorithm.* [online] Wikipedia. Available at: https://en.wikipedia.org/wiki/Algorithm.

4.   du Sautoy, M. (2020). *The creativity code: Art and innovation in the age of AI.* Cambridge, MA: Belknap Harvard.

5.   Walch, K. (n.d.). *Artificial intelligence is not a technology.* [online] Forbes. Available at: https://www.forbes.com/sites/cognitiveworld/2018/11/01/artificial-intelligence-is-not-a-technology/#:~:text=AI%20is%20not%20a%20technology [Accessed 7 Aug. 2021].

6.   News18. (2020). *Elon Musk thinks that artificial intelligence will be "vastly smarter" than humans in 5 years.* [online] News18. Available at:

https://www.news18.com/news/buzz/elon-musk-thinks-that-artificial-intelligence-will-be-vastly-smarter-than-humans-in-5-years-2741359.html [Accessed 7 Aug. 2021].

7. Latar, N.L. and Nordfors, D. (2011). *The future of journalism: Artificial intelligence and digital identities.* [online] CiteSeerX. Available at: http://citeseerx.ist.psu.edu/viewdoc/download?doi=10.1.1.458.7543&rep=rep1&type=pdf [Accessed 2 Jun. 2001].

8. Vad Jesperson, H. (2020). *What is AI? — AI terminology.* [online] Raptor. Available at: https://www.raptorservices.com/what-is-ai-ai-terminology/#:~:text=value%20and%20applicability. [Accessed 7 Aug. 2021].

9. Sterne, J. (2017). *Artificial intelligence for marketing: practical applications.* Hoboken, NJ: Wiley.

10. Sterne, J. (2017). *Artificial intelligence for marketing: practical applications.* Hoboken, NJ: Wiley.

11. Ethics of AI (n.d.). *What is transparency? Ethics of AI.* [online] Ethics of AI. Available at: https://ethics-of-ai.mooc.fi/chapter-4/2-what-is-transparency [Accessed 7 Aug. 2021].

12. Ford, M. (2016). *Rise of the robots: technology and the threat of a jobless future.* New York, NY: Basic Books.

13. Condor Ferries. (n.d.). *100+ plastic in the ocean statistics & facts (2020).* [online] Condor Ferries. Available at: https://www.condorferries.co.uk/plastic-in-the-ocean-statistics#:~:text=Every%20day%20around%208%20milli on.

14. bluevision. (2019). *Artificial intelligence and robots may solve recycling crisis.* [online] bluevision Available at: https://bluevisionbraskem.com/en/innovation/artificial-intelligence-and-robots-may-solve-recycling-crisis/ [Accessed 7 Aug. 2021].

15. bluevision. (2019). *Artificial intelligence and robots may solve recycling crisis.* [online] bluevision Available at: https://bluevisionbraskem.com/en/innovation/artificial-intelligence-and-robots-may-solve-recycling-crisis/ [Accessed 7 Aug. 2021].

16. Al-Nasser, N. (2020). *Will AI replace the majority of jobs?* [online] Medium. Available at: https://medium.com/@nadiaalnasser28/will-ai-replace-the-majority-21ce5e13c533 [Accessed 7 Aug. 2021].

17. Bregman, R. (2018). *Utopia for realists.* London; New York, NY: Bloomsbury.

18. Valin, J. (2018). *Humans still needed: An analysis of skills and tools in public relations.* [online] CIPR. Available at: https://www.researchgate.net/publication/325344241_ Humans_still_needed_An_analysis_of_skills_and_tools_ in_public_relations [Accessed 5 Feb. 2021].

19. Bregman, R. (2018). *Utopia for Realists.* London; New York, NY: Bloomsbury.

20. Valin, J. (2018). *Humans still needed: An analysis of skills and tools in public relations.* [online] CIPR. Available at: https://www.researchgate.net/publication/325344241_ Humans_still_needed_An_analysis_of_skills_and_tools_ in_public_relations [Accessed 5 Feb. 2021].

21. Sterne, J. (2017). *Artificial intelligence for marketing: practical applications.* Hoboken, NJ: Wiley.

22. Tiraboschi, L. (2018). *The ketchup effect.* [online] Impactscool Magazine. Available at: https://magazine.impactscool.com/en/robotica-e-ai/the-ketchup-effetc/.

23. Kowalczyk, P. (2013). *On this computer the first ebook in the world was created.* [online] Ebook Friendly. Available at: https://ebookfriendly.com/computer-first-ebook-was-created/#:~:text=Declaration%20of%20Independence%2 C%20the%20first [Accessed 7 Aug. 2021].

24. *BBC News. (2012). Amazon selling more Kindle ebooks than print books.* [online] BBC News. Available at: https://www.bbc.co.uk/news/technology-19148146.

25. Susskind, R. (2019). *Future of the professions: how technology will transform the work of human experts, updated... edition.* Oxford: Oxford University Press.

26. Susskind, R. (2019). *Future of the professions: how technology will transform the work of human experts, updated... edition.* Oxford: Oxford University Press.

27. Susskind, R. (2019). *Future of the professions: how technology will transform the work of human experts, updated... edition.* Oxford: Oxford University Press.

28. Holiday, R. (2018*). Trust me, I'm lying: Confessions of a media manipulator.* New York, NY: Profile Books.

29. Gruner, D. T., and Csikszentmihalyi, M. (2019). *The Palgrave handbook of social creativity research.* New York, NY: Springer.

30. Kasparov, G.K. and Greengard, M. (2018). *Deep thinking: where machine intelligence ends and human creativity begins.* London: John Murray.

31. du Sautoy, M. (2020). *The creativity code: Art and innovation in the age of AI.* Cambridge, MA: Belknap Harvard.

32. Johnson, G. (2016). *To beat Go champion, Google's program needed a human army.* [online] The New York Times. Available at: https://www.nytimes.com/2016/04/05/science/google-alphago-artificial-intelligence.html [Accessed 7 Aug. 2021].

33. Silver, D. and Hassabis, D. (2018). *AlphaGo Zero: Starting from scratch.* [online] DeepMind. Available at: https://deepmind.com/blog/article/alphago-zero-starting-scratch

34. Harari, Y. N. (2018). *Homo deus: a brief history of tomorrow.* New York, NY: Harper Perennial.

35. Criddle, C. (2021). *"Self-driving" cars to be allowed on UK roads this year.* [online] BBC News. Available at: https://www.bbc.co.uk/news/technology-56906145.

36. Youn, S. (2019). *UPS joins race for future of delivery services by investing in self-driving trucks.* [online] ABC News. Available at: https://abcnews.go.com/Business/ups-joins-race-future-delivery-services-investing-driving/story?id=65014414.

37. Columbus, L. and Columbus, L. (2019). *10 charts that will change your perspective of AI in marketing.* [online] Cloud Tech. Available at: https://www.cloudcomputing-news.net/news/2019/jul/15/10-charts-that-will-change-

your-perspective-of-ai-in-marketing/ [Accessed 10 Nov. 2019].

38. Valin, J. (2019). *An introduction to AI in PR, skills guide.* [online] CIPR. Available at: https://www.cipr.co.uk/sites/default/files/Intro_to_AI.pdf [Accessed 10 Nov. 2019].

39. Sterne, J. (2017). *Artificial intelligence for marketing: practical applications.* Hoboken, NJ: Wiley.

40. Sterne, J. (2017). *Artificial intelligence for marketing: practical applications.* Hoboken, NJ: Wiley.

41. Carr, N. (2015). *The glass cage: Automation and us.* New York, NY: W. W. Norton & Company.

42. Sterne, J. (2017). *Artificial intelligence for marketing: practical applications.* Hoboken, NJ: Wiley.

43. Carr, N. (2015). *The glass cage: Automation and us.* New York, NY: W. W. Norton & Company.

44. Carr, N. (2015). *The glass cage: Automation and us.* New York, NY: W. W. Norton & Company.

45. Carr, N. (2015). *The glass cage: Automation and us.* New York, NY: W. W. Norton & Company.

46. Woodyard, C. (2014). *Toyota replacing robots with people.* [online] USA Today. Available at: https://eu.usatoday.com/story/driveon/2014/04/08/toyota-robots-workers-efficiency/7463269/ [Accessed 7 Aug. 2021].

47. Harari, Y. N. (2014). *Will people still be useful in the 21st century?* [online] CNN. Available at: https://edition.cnn.com/2014/09/17/opinion/opinion-tomorrow-transformed-harari/index.html#:~:text=The%20idea%20that%20humans%20will [Accessed 7 Aug. 2021].

48. Dawkins, R. (2016). *The god delusion.* London: Black Swan.

49. Harari, Y. N. (2018). *Homo deus: a brief history of tomorrow.* New York, NY: Harper Perennial.

50. Fish, T. (2020). *GlastonburAI: Recreate Glasto 2020 headline acts at home thanks to artificial intelligence.* [online] The Express. Available at: https://www.express.co.uk/news/science/1301357/glastonbury-2020-artificial-intelligence-recreate-glasto-2020-headline-music [Accessed 7 Aug. 2021].

51. Williamson, V. (2013). *The science of music: Why do songs in a minor key sound sad?* [online] NME. Available at: https://www.nme.com/blogs/nme-blogs/the-science-of-music-why-do-songs-in-a-minor-key-sound-sad-760215.

52. Fauvel, J., Flood, R. and Wilson, R. J. (2008). *Music and mathematics: from Pythagoras to fractals.* Oxford: Oxford University Press.

53. da Silva, P. (2010). *Interview with composer David Cope: Part I.* [online] The Sound Stew. Available at: http://www.thesoundstew.com/2010/07/interview-with-david-cope.html.

54. Ford, M. (2016). *Rise of the robots: technology and the threat of a jobless future.* New York, NY: Basic Books.

55. Susskind, R. (2019). *Future of the professions: how technology will transform the work of human experts, updated... edition.* Oxford: Oxford University Press.

56. du Sautoy, M. (2020). *The creativity code: art and innovation in the age of AI.* Cambridge, MA: Belknap Harvard.

57. Smith, A. (2014). *What do clients really want from their PR agencies?* [online] PRmoment. Available at: https://www.prmoment.com/pr-insight/what-do-clients-really-want-from-their-pr-agencies [Accessed 8 Aug. 2021].

58. BBC News. (2015). *Ada Lovelace: Letters shed light on tech visionary.* [online]BBC News. Available at:

https://www.bbc.co.uk/news/science-environment-34243042 [Accessed 8 Aug. 2021].

59. du Sautoy, M. (2020). *The creativity code: art and innovation in the age of AI.* Cambridge, MA: Belknap Harvard.

60. Rushkoff, D. (2021). *Team human.* New York, NY: W. W. Norton & Company.

61. Colton, S., Pantic, M. and Valstar, M. (2007). *Emotionally aware portraiture.* [online] The Painting Fool. Available at: http://www.thepaintingfool.com/galleries/emotionally_aware/index.html [Accessed 7 Aug. 2021].

62. du Sautoy, M. (2020). *The creativity code: art and innovation in the age of AI.* Cambridge, MA: Belknap Harvard.

63. IBM Cloud Education. (2020). *What is supervised learning?* [online] IBM. Available at: https://www.ibm.com/cloud/learn/supervised-learning.

64. Gruner, D. T., and Csikszentmihalyi, M. (2019). *The Palgrave handbook of social creativity research.* New York, NY: Springer.

65. Boden, M. A. (1998). *Creativity and artificial intelligence. A contradiction in terms?* [online]

Ruskin.TV. Available at:
http://www.ruskin.tv/maggieb/downloads/Artificial_In
telligence_and_Creativity__Contradiction_in_Terms__.
pdf.pdf.

66. du Sautoy, M. (2020). *The creativity code: art and innovation in the age of AI.* Cambridge, MA: Belknap Harvard.

67. Enos, M. (2018). *In defense of "Revolution 9" at 50: Why the Beatles' most daring track is still underrated.* [online] Billboard. Available at:
https://www.billboard.com/articles/columns/r
ock/8486236/the-beatles-revolution-9-white-
album-defense.

68. Boden, M. A. (1998). *Creativity and artificial intelligence. A contradiction in terms?* [online] Ruskin.TV. Available at:
http://www.ruskin.tv/maggieb/downloads/Artificial_In
telligence_and_Creativity__Contradiction_in_Terms__.
pdf.pdf.

69. Boden, M. A. (1998). *Creativity and artificial intelligence. A contradiction in terms?* [online] Ruskin.TV. Available at:
http://www.ruskin.tv/maggieb/downloads/Artificial_In
telligence_and_Creativity__Contradiction_in_Terms__.
pdf.pdf.

70. Boden, M. A. (1998). *Creativity and artificial intelligence. A contradiction in terms?* [online] Ruskin.TV. Available at: http://www.ruskin.tv/maggieb/downloads/Artificial_Intelligence_and_Creativity__Contradiction_in_Terms__. pdf.pdf.

71. du Sautoy, M. (2020). *The creativity code: art and innovation in the age of AI.* Cambridge, MA: Belknap Harvard.

72. du Sautoy, M. (2020). *The creativity code: art and innovation in the age of AI.* Cambridge, MA.: Belknap Harvard.

73. Ingham, F. (2019). *PR and communications census 2019.* [online] PRCA. Available at: https://www.prca.org.uk/sites/default/files/PRCA_PR_Census_2019_v9-8-pdf%20%285%29.pdf [Accessed Aug. 2AD].

74. Ford, M. (2016). *Rise of the robots: technology and the threat of a jobless future.* New York, NY: Basic Books.

75. Barlow, N. (2016). *Love letters sent by Manchester's baby.* [online] About Manchester. Available at: https://aboutmanchester.co.uk/love-letters-sent-by-manchesters-baby/ [Accessed 7 Aug. 2021].

76. du Sautoy, M. (2020). *The creativity code: art and innovation in the age of AI.* Cambridge, MA: Belknap Harvard.

77. Kurzweil CyberArt Technologies. (2001). Kurzweil CyberArt Technologies. [online] Kurzweil CyberArt Technologies. Available at: http://www.kurzweilcyberart.com/poetry/rkcp_overvie w.php [Accessed 7 Aug. 2021].

78. Cheil, E. (2014). *Want to make a bot that'll write a novel? November is the time to do it.* [online] WNYC Studios. Available at: https://www.wnycstudios.org/podcasts/otm/articles/wa nt-make-bot-ll-write-novel-november-time-do-it [Accessed 7 Aug. 2021].

79. Johnson, K. (2020). *OpenAI debuts gigantic GPT-3 language model with 175 billion parameters.* [online] VentureBeat. Available at: https://venturebeat.com/2020/05/29/openai-debuts-gigantic-gpt-3-language-model-with-175-billion-parameters/ [Accessed 7 Aug. 2021].

80. Douglas Heaven, W. (2020). *OpenAI's new language generator GPT-3 is shockingly good—and completely mindless.* [online] MIT Technology Review. Available at: https://www.technologyreview.com/2020/07/20/10054 54/openai-machine-learning-language-generator-gpt-3-nlp/.

81. GPT-3. (2020). *A robot wrote this entire article. Are you scared yet, human?* [online} The Guardian. Available at: https://www.theguardian.com/commentisfree/2020/sep/08/robot-wrote-this-article-gpt-3.

82. Sterne, J. (2017). *Artificial intelligence for marketing: practical applications.* Hoboken, NJ: Wiley.

83. Youngmann, B., Gilad-Bachrach, R., Yom-Tov, E. and Karmon, D. (2019). *The automated copywriter: Algorithmic rephrasing of health-related advertisements to improve their performance.* [ebook] New York, NY: Cornell University. Available at: https://arxiv.org/pdf/1910.12274.pdf [Accessed 10 Nov. 2019].

84. du Sautoy, M. (2020). *The creativity code: art and innovation in the age of AI.* Cambridge, MA: Belknap Harvard.

85. du Sautoy, M. (2020). *The creativity code: art and innovation in the age of AI.* Cambridge, MA: Belknap Harvard.

86. WashPostPR. (2016). *The Washington Post to use artificial intelligence to cover nearly 500 races on election day.* [online] Washington Post. Available at: https://www.washingtonpost.com/pr/wp/2016/10/19/the-washington-post-uses-artificial-intelligence-to-cover-

nearly-500-races-on-election-day/ [Accessed 7 Aug. 2021].

87. Waleed, A. and Hassoun, M. (2019). *Artificial intelligence and automated journalism: Contemporary challenges and new opportunities.* International Journal of Media, Journalism and Mass Communications, 5(1).

88. Dakin-White, J. (2018). *How can AI help PR professionals do a better job right now?* [online] Wildfire. Available at: https://www.wildfirepr.com/blog/i-tried-failed-write-press-release-ai-machine-learning/ [Accessed 7 Aug. 2021].

89. Zyro (n.d.). *AI content generator – Generate quality content for your site.* [online] Zyro. Available at: https://zyro.com/ai/content-generator.

90. Tillman, M. (2021). *What is Google Duplex and how does it work?* [online] Pocket-lint. Available at: https://www.pocket-lint.com/phones/news/google/146008-what-is-google-duplex-where-is-it-available-and-how-does-it-work

91. BBC News. (2020). *Microsoft "to replace journalists with robots."* [online] BBC News. Available at: https://www.bbc.co.uk/news/world-us-canada-52860247 [Accessed 7 Aug. 2021].

92. Nahser, F. (2018). *Automating BuzzFeed.* [online] Medium. Available at: https://medium.com/global-editors-network/automating-buzzfeed-bcbdb472bdc4 [Accessed 8 Aug. 2021].

93. Fedeli, S., Grieco, E. and Sumida, N. (2018). *About a third of large U.S. newspapers have suffered layoffs since 2017.* [online] Pew Research Center. Available at: https://www.pewresearch.org/fact-tank/2018/07/23/about-a-third-of-large-u-s-newspapers-have-suffered-layoffs-since-2017/ [Accessed 14 Oct. 2020].

94. Wood, P. (2020). *News UK set to cut jobs in radio and newspaper.* [online] City A.M. Available at: https://www.cityam.com/news-uk-set-to-cut-jobs-in-radio-and-newspaper/ [Accessed 8 Aug. 2021].

95. Verma, S. (2021). *Burnout makes journalists quit jobs and the pandemic is not the only reason.* [online] The Citizen. Available at: https://www.thecitizen.in/index.php/en/newsdetail/index/14/20709/burnout-makes-journalists-quit-jobs-and-the-pandemic-is-not-the-only-reason [Accessed 9 Aug. 2021].

96. Schneider, M. (2018). *Report: PR pros outnumber journalists by a 6-to-1 ratio.* [online] PR Daily. Available at: https://www.prdaily.com/report-pr-pros-outnumber-

journalists-by-a-6-to-1-ratio/ [Accessed 7 Aug. 2021].

97. Forbes Councils. (n.d.). [online] Forbes Councils. Available at: https://councils.forbes.com/ [Accessed 7 Aug. 2021].

98. Rushkoff, D. (2021). *Team human.* New York, NY: W. W Norton & Company.

99. Susskind, R. (2019). *Future of the professions: how technology will transform the work of human experts, updated... edition.* Oxford: Oxford University Press.